FORGED FROM THE FIRE
BORN IN HELL

A MEMOIR

MY JOURNEY FROM NIHILISM TO CHRISTIANITY

Jack Flynn

Published by Jack Flynn, 2021.

While every precaution has been taken in the preparation of this book, the publisher assumes no responsibility for errors or omissions, or for damages resulting from the use of the information contained herein.

FORGED FROM THE FIRE BORN IN HELL A MEMOIR MY JOURNEY FROM NIHILISM TO CHRISTIANITY

First edition. February 19, 2021.

Written by Jack Flynn.

I deadicate my memoir to Mia, my beautiful daughter, whom I love dearly.

Chapter 1—Haunted House

One particular day I was in my room. I suddenly heard crashing and banging upstairs and the dull thump of bone hitting flesh. Yelling and screaming erupted, and instantly my body took over. I guess I felt like it was time.

My head was completely confused and terrified while my body rushed upstairs. I did a very taboo move by opening the door to my parents' room. When I got into the room, I saw my mother with her clothes torn and my father standing over her. I wanted the fighting to stop. I was trying to explain to my dad that what he was doing is wrong. As I talked, he was looking a bit surprised. As I continued talking, Mom ran out the door behind me, and then a moment later we heard the front door close.

My father was never listening to me; I just broke his usual rhythm. The moment the door closed, he ran after Mom as if I weren't even in the room. In a fit of rage, I smashed everything in sight—lamps, tables, chairs, etc. Then I ran out of the house after my father. When I got to them, my mother was sitting on the curb, crying, with the beast looming over her.

The beast turned to see me boldly walk up to the scene. I guess he could see that I was out of line, because he challenged me with a dare. He leaned his face forward and asked, "What are you gonna do, boy?" I stood bewildered and confused. He asked, "You gonna hit me, boy?" It must have been written all over my face, even though I didn't feel it.

The beast pointed to his face and said, "Go ahead, hit me!" Fifteen years of rage and fear boiled over. I was terrified, so I hit him with everything I had. I had seen many people hit my father and get pounded for it. I was terrified that he might be invincible. So I held nothing back.

After I hit him, he moved in to grab me—or so I thought. His weight crashed in on me, and I struggled to hold onto him, when I instead just let him go and stepped aside. He fell to the ground with a thump. He lay there, not moving. He was out cold.

My mother made her way to her sister's house, and after a minute the beast wobbled to his feet. He was missing his glasses, and his eye was already beginning to swell shut. He started back toward the house with the parting words that we would finish this in the house. I immediately went after him and followed him until I stopped at our driveway. He went on into the house, and at that moment right there, I decided to leave home for a few weeks. I was afraid my dad would shoot me if I went in after him.

As far back as I can remember, I have known violence. As a small child, there were some very quick lessons I learned about the world in order to survive. The beast called "Father" was in absolute control of me and my world. My life revolved around this beast.

Father expected everything to be done perfectly, and for some reason my tiny hands and feet failed to be perfect. I was obviously the problem here, because I was always disappointing Father. Father always looked at me with contempt and disgust, as if I were the root of all his agony.

Over time, I got pretty good at being invisible. I made a very small footprint everywhere I went so I would not disturb the beast. I became almost perfect at hiding, sneaking, and not disturbing anything around me—although it was as if the whole floor of the house was made of thin ice.

I was not the only one living in the prison camp. My fellow prisoners who were closest to me seemed to mess up more than me. My fellow prisoners, or "sisters," as they are called by many, would disturb things more than me because they had to take care of their appearance. They were always in the bathroom where Father also went. I was terrified because it was inevitable that something of his would be disturbed and violence would erupt.

At this point I had read many a comic book, and I wanted to be a hero like the strong, brave warriors I read about. This caused a lot of problems for me. More than anything in the world, I wanted to be a warrior for good.

Inevitably, my sisters would disturb the beast's sacred objects—such as a comb. Or even worse, someone would put the toilet paper on the roll backwards. This infuriated the beast into a raging frenzy. Everyone was terrified of him, so no one would admit who did the terrible deed.

The beast would then send us into a bedroom and tell us to send out the guilty party or else we would all equally be terrorized and beaten. I, being the brave little hero I was, looked at my sisters' tender skin, shiny hair, and small stature as weakness. Even though they were older than me, I decided it was my duty as a brave warrior for good to face the beast on their behalf. I would rescue them even though it was never my fault. We talked it out in the bedroom, and my sisters were relieved to see I was going to be horribly and mercilessly beaten and not them. I bravely walked straight into the beast's arms for my unwarranted punishment.

The delighted and now smug beast would seize his leather whip from its holster. With an absolute sense of righteousness and rage, he would begin to rain down blow after blow on my tiny body. I hated being so small. Why do I have to be so small and weak?

The beast would yell that he was going to beat me until the blood ran, which made me think that surely, this time, he was going to finally kill me. I would involuntarily throw my arms up to block the blows, and my fingers would turn numb when they came in contact with the whip. My body would be writhing in agony from the stinging fire raining down on me.

The beast would howl in rage that I had dared to block the blows. Father then would command me to hold my arms over my head until he was done beating me. If I did not, he threatened to beat me even harder.

In a haze of stabbing pain and humiliation, I would bravely keep my hands aloft until the beating had ceased. Through tear-soaked eyes and snot, I would keep my gaze on my torturer just as he commanded. When he was finally done beating me, with his teeth clinched in disgust, he would force out the words, "You will never take my comb out of the bathroom again!" I could tell he was quite satisfied with the results. My body burning with welts that were just beginning to appear, I would go hide in the closet, holding my breath, too terrified to make a sound for fear of him coming back.

This went on countless times for seemingly endless scenarios. I was such a horrible little boy for being such a pain to my father. There is something horribly wrong with me to be treated so. I am bad, rotten, and useless from the start. Hopeless. What is a little boy to do?

The beast's mate was as much a weakling as me. She was really of no use against the beast because she actually served him and chased after him. I saw this woman as a slave like the rest of us, only for some terrifying reason she worshiped the beast as well.

Most of the time, the gypsy woman who lived with us was not around. She would tell me that Daddy didn't mean to hurt me. Then she would go about singing as if nothing was happening. She was hollow and devoid of substance. She was an apparition that would visit me from time to time to sing and dance an animated, colorful, fantastic carnival of distraction.

She waited hand and foot on the beast. When she fed him, he would oversee her every move and painstakingly scrutinize her actions. It was inevitable there would be a problem. If she gave him a fork he disapproved of, in an act of showing his supremacy, he would bend the fork in half and throw it across the room, demanding she replace it.

This is where the woman would actually provoke the beast. She would get him a fork and then tell the beast, with contempt, what a jerk he was. Words would be exchanged, and the beast would attack the woman. In a fury of flesh-cracking, jumbled screaming, they would go to the floor, wrestling and punching. My little mind could not grasp why this woman would self-mutilate like this.

At this point, the food I was already choking down with a dry throat would seize in place. My body would strangle me out of terror. Frozen in place, unable to move, I would stare at the horror show, believing this woman was the only thing standing between me and certain pain and death.

Surreal madness would then arrive, and my father would calmly sit back in his chair at the dinner table looking victorious and righteous. With a gloating smirk and very controlled, slow movements to accentuate how much control he had, he would return to eating. My mother, with her clothes torn and her makeup running from tears, would return to whatever it was she had been doing before the eruption.

I sat, confused, terrified, and perplexed, unable to move for fear of drawing the beast's attention to me. I was secretly glad the woman hadn't been killed, because I was next. Mother was very beautiful, yet she was a strange mix of self-punishing, masochistic desires. My fellow prisoners and I would then move to please the beast as best we could, because that's what Mother did to survive.

Obviously, I lived to serve this monster, and I hated him. To keep the hatred from being discovered, I would run interference by being overly nice and serving to him. I was disgusted, helpless, and terrified.

I had four fellow prisoners who were called brothers and sisters. I had two older male siblings and two older female siblings. I was the youngest of the prisoners to this beast.

I did have safe places that I would seek out as often as possible. I never felt safe in the house. I would go down to the creek that wasn't far across the corn fields that surrounded our Midwestern home. The land was flat, and I could see for miles and miles to the horizon. There would be a thicket of trees here and there. The fields of soy beans and corn went on until they disappeared where the land met the huge sky overhead.

There was an ominous structure I could see in the distance. It was a prison farm. I knew it was a dangerous place because of how people talked about it. But down by the creek I felt free to exercise my imagination. I would go to wonderful lands where I would battle evil and rescue the slaves. I would be by myself for hours at a time. My imagination was the only place I could move about with no fear.

I did struggle with a recurring nightmare. I was always running in slow motion from a beast. The crushing helplessness drowned me, as I could never seem to get away. The terrifying beast was always searching for me and always had the upper hand. It knew my every thought. Hopelessly, I struggled on in vain to evade the monster.

We never missed a sermon on Sundays. We had great church attendance. Sunday mornings have always been a terrible time for me. My father would wake us all up and begin a verbal countdown as to when we should be in the car. Every five minutes he would announce the time that the car was pulling out. "Twenty minutes to departure," he would threaten. I knew there would be violence if I did not comply.

Terrified, I would try to get ready while fighting my body, which was resisting me. Frustrated, I would push through my limbs which were seizing up on me. I didn't understand it. I felt exhausted, and I couldn't think straight. I was angry at my weakness. I hated being weak.

My dad despised me on Sundays. He was angry that I couldn't properly dress myself. He would call me a lazy bum and say that I would never amount to anything. I was frustrated that I couldn't meet his expectations. I hated myself because I was such an awful and difficult child.

The beast would yell, scream, and threaten us all the way to the church parking lot. When we parked and got out of the car, my father would change. He would begin to smile, I knew he was a beast, yet he would start smiling and pretending. I was terrified of everyone and everything because I figured this is the way everyone lived. When together in public, people would do the surreal dance of harmony. I believed that everyone lived like we did. People were very scary, strange, and unfamiliar to me.

When it came to God, I heard his name spoken much of the time with a look of reverence. Everyone seemed to believe in God. Both my grandmas spoke of him regularly. My dad never talked about Him much, but I could tell when he did it was to say we better acknowledge Jesus in our lives, or else God was going to get us in a bad way. My mother never talked about Jesus.

We went to church religiously. My dad saw it as something extremely important. No matter what happened, I needed to be at church. I remember looking at a picture of this figure called "Jesus" on the wall at the tiny rural Baptist church we attended. Jesus was holding a baby lamb in his arms, and he had a gentle smile. Jesus looked like a nice enough man, but what a weakling. I was not impressed. He looked wimpy and anemic. The beast could easily have pummeled him. I hated the beast, but I had respect for him, like one would have respect for a rattlesnake on a foot trail.

My family and relatives talked about Jesus and used him with reverence in every other word, yet there was only emptiness in their words. His name was used with little effect. It just seemed a dull, uninteresting part of the social landscape. When the name of Jesus was spoken, it was a compulsory nod to an invisible karma. It was as though if you didn't use his name, something bad would happen; it was a strange exercise in redundancy, meaningless.

For a time, my family changed churches and went to one in the city. This is when I first felt the presence of God. I don't remember the sermon or even who the pastor was. I was very young, maybe six years old.

It was a very simple transaction between me and Jesus. The pastor said that Jesus was good, perfectly good. Jesus was good and mankind killed him for this. Jesus wants the world to be happy, yet the world denied him and killed him. I felt terrible for Jesus. I wanted him to know I loved him. I told Jesus I was sorry and I wanted to be a part of his good plan for the world. I wanted the world to be happy, too.

A void in my life was somehow filled in that moment when I reached out to receive Jesus. I was so excited that I went to tell my parents the good news about Jesus saving me. They didn't want any part of the message I had received about love overcoming evil. I told my father that if he would learn to love people, we could all be happy. The beast didn't want happiness. I was very disappointed and confused.

At first I was very excited about Jesus Christ and what he had done. Yet, over time, nothing changed. The beast kept abusing all of us, and Mom was just as aloof and cold as ever. An avalanche of darkness fell back over me and I lost that beautiful moment with Jesus. Jesus was powerless to help me and my family. What a shame.

The violence continued outside the home from a bully. In first grade, I was singled out by Lamont Trickle. He hated how I was trying so hard to be friendly with my new first grade classmates. He started mocking me straightaway. The mocking turned into threats. I was scared, but I knew what brave warriors would do. They would confront bad people, so I did.

Some of the new friends I made invited me to play over at their house. I came with my toy trucks to share with them. I was very afraid when Lamont stepped out from behind a tree. It was a trap. My new friends had betrayed me. Lamont bullied me, intimidated me, and threatened me. We never physically fought, because I stood my ground and waited for him to attack. He never did, but I was terrified.

Chapter 2—Southern Hospitality

When I turned nine years old, the violence in my life surged. For whatever reason, my parents decided to move to Houston, Texas. It was 1981 when we moved. I went from a small, humble, classic school in the Midwest to what seemed like an outer space colony of the future. It was a shock. The buildings and architecture of Houston were overwhelmingly huge and shiny. Everything seemed to be chrome, glass, and cement. The schools were brand new and painted with bright colors. I had never seen anything like it.

We lived in Texas in the early 80s. We lived a "feast or famine" life. One day we would be living in a new, air-conditioned home in a nice suburb. The next, we were living out of a car or in a boarded-up condemned home.

We would live without electricity or water for weeks at a time. I hated that I had to lie on my parents' behalf to debt collectors and landlords. It was humiliating and terrifying.

The violence at home continued. My father would still beat up Mom. Occasionally Dad had to be bailed out of jail for fighting someone or defying a policeman. I hated that my mother would bail him out. It was exasperating to watch her help him.

Meanwhile, I had to walk through the neighborhoods we lived in to get to school. For a time I went to school in the barrio. The barrio was a particularly bad neighborhood full of gangs and drug activity. It wasn't easy being the only white, red-headed kid in a Mexican neighborhood.

In my mind at the time, there was no one to turn to. I only had myself. The cops were not an option, because I grew up with a dad con-

9

stantly telling me how these horrible, power-hungry policemen would pick on him out of nowhere. I remember them taking my dad away many times. My mother hated them as well.

The beast was certainly not an option. I was terrified of my father, and I tried to avoid him at every turn. It never even entered my mind to tell my mother, because she was helpless. I was scared of everybody, and I trusted no one. No authorities could be trusted—not teachers, principals, no one.

Each morning I would walk down the street with front yards made of dirt where hostile kids were waiting on me. The only thing I had was my code. I had an honor code. I think I picked it up from reading Conan the Barbarian comics and watching John Wayne movies and Kung Fu Action Theater every Saturday on the TV. I learned how a good warrior was supposed to be—brave in the face of danger.

Running away, hiding, or sneaking was never an option. That was the option for cowards. I lived the "death before dishonor" code. I truly lived that code out on those violent streets. Every day I walked down the same street, the same way, and every day five to seven Mexican kids were waiting to attack me and beat me down.

I never won a fight on the street with so many, but I didn't believe there was any way to avoid it. I fought and fought and fought. I never gave up. I fought until they got tired of beating on me. Then they would move on, and I would go to school with clothes torn and cuts bleeding. The worse part, to me, wasn't the physical pain. It was the humiliation of losing the fight.

Then recess came. It would all happen all over again, only they would attack me with professional wrestling moves to make it look like we were playing. In my mind, there was no help. I was completely alone.

On the way home from school, the attacks continued. I was never going to hide or run because, to me, dishonor was a fate worse than death. Fighting became a part of the landscape. It wasn't so bad. I was a chunky, slow kid. I was not a great fighter. I could take a beating, though.

Fighting became a boundary for me. I had been in a lot of fights. I was the new kid at a school, sometimes twice in a year. We would move houses regularly.

My dad would quit his job or get fired. He ran out of money, so we had to move. He would regularly say how much he hated his job and how horrible his bosses were. He was always a victim to some horrible person. The grownup world looked like a horrible, bleak place.

We were evicted by the sheriff also. The sheriff and his deputies came into the house and threw all of our belongings on the curb next to the street. My mother would remark that they were horrible people and that they were just being mean. I was terrified of the police.

We still never missed one day of church after we moved to Texas. Sunday was horrible because it was the one day I could not avoid my father. The beast was always most terrifying on Sundays.

It was when I was walking to school one morning that I first saw porn. There was a colorful magazine page lying on the ground. I reached down, picked it up, and saw the most beautiful thing I had ever seen in my life.

The most wonderful, euphoric feeling came over my body as I gazed at the beautiful naked girl. I felt so deeply flattered that this girl would show me her most intimate side. I fell in love. It was love at first sight, for sure. I lived in a world of loneliness and rejection. This made me feel wonderful.

I knew right away that it was wrong. A moment later I balled up the paper and threw it down, although it was too late. All the crushing pain I was in had subsided, if only for a brief moment. As soon as school was out, like a starving person, I hurried back to where I had thrown down the angel. She was gone. I couldn't find her. It made me feel even more sad and alone. I needed her.

For her to show me this intimate side of herself—it made me feel accepted, connected, complete, and safe. Like a loving, accepting mother, she cradled me in her arms and made everything right in my life, if only for a moment. My undernourished, empty heart was starving for intimacy. I was hopelessly smitten.

Chapter 3—Out of the Frying Pan ...

After we bounced around Houston for three years, my parents moved us to northern Virginia. We came in the spring. Virginia was absolutely beautiful. In the spring it seemed as if every bush and tree had a brilliant color. Flowers were in bloom everywhere. And the trees—it was as if the people built a city in a thick forest but did not disturb a single tree. There were so many trees that it seemed as if they would overrun the roads at any time. It was wonderful.

The house we moved into was in a very expensive neighborhood. My dad got another mechanic job, and my mother worked for the airlines. We were on top financially, I guess.

Of course, I had to start a new school again. I was terrified of everyone and I was hopelessly a loner. I had to ride the school bus for the first time since I had lived in the Midwest. The first day to ride the bus I remember the terrifying walk to the bus stop where there was a group of kids. It was right across the street from my house.

There was a small side street where several kids gathered to wait. I pushed myself through what seemed to be an invisible barrier. My heart was in my throat and I was sweating. I stopped short on the corner right across the small street. I froze. I couldn't go any further, so that's where I stayed. I felt humiliated. I was too scared to join the others, so that's where I stood the rest of the year while waiting for the bus—on the far corner.

I knew it was weird, but my social anxiety was too great to overcome. The only time I would say anything to them is when they would all ask me in unison what time it was. I was glad I had a watch. This gave me some dignity. They called me "Juice" because I frequently wore an 80s shirt that had these words splashed in color across the front.

The fights started all over again. I was the new kid and stayed to myself, which made me a target. At recess, a huge bully would show up and begin to try to humiliate me. I would stand up for myself, and then I would be attacked from all sides by his friends. I always fought and never gave up until we were separated by a teacher.

At this point, I had learned some tricks for fighting a group of kids. I started to hold my own. I could take a hit, but I started to be able to give a hit as well. I won some fights and lost others. This is how I met a character named Sammy Hill. At first he was one of the kids heckling me from the sideline of gathered students who wanted to watch the new kid get beat up. After I started to win, though, he joined me and made friends with me. This is the type of person I considered a friend because I really had no discernment for kids who were mean but not physically trying to hurt me.

I was a naive kid, so I believe Sammy saw me as more of a mascot than a friend. I was hurting for a friend and so I partnered with this mixed bag of joker, antagonist, and prankster. He was quite a devilish imp.

Sammy was busting at the seams for adventure. He was very enthusiastic and physically active. He was constantly getting into trouble. This made him very exciting. I got into throwing eggs or water balloons at cars and snow balls at the drunken college kids when they came out of the bars. This got Sammy beat up sometimes, but that was part of the excitement.

Sammy challenged my beliefs much like the Devil would. I didn't cuss. It was taboo in my family. He pushed and pushed until I finally caved in because I had no good answer. He was right. There was no good reason why. So I opened with a tirade of curse words on the basketball court one day. I believe Sammy loved corrupting me. I came to do many new illegal things with Sammy throughout the years.

His parents were never around, so we had that in common. We ran the streets with no supervision. His parents were very wealthy, and they lived in an historical district. His family was deeply southern and they had the accents to prove it.

We finished elementary school together but when we got to middle school, he started going to a private school. We still got together quite often, though. I chased after him and put up with his treating me like a second-class citizen for the adventure. He was quite a snob, and he was quick to point out how poor and pathetic I was. I guess I put up with it because of the crushing shame I lived with. I believed what he said about me. I felt as if I deserved it. I didn't like it, but I also didn't have the self-respect to challenge him.

Sammy introduced me to his parents' extensive liquor cabinet. Oh joy! What an amazing elixir we would put together with the plethora of choices! Alcohol was a game-changer for me socially and emotionally. I hated the taste of alcohol, but I drank for one purpose only—to get completely hammered.

When I was wasted, the world was what it should be. I felt light as a feather because the ten-thousand-pound weight of helplessness and social awkwardness was completely lifted. I was quite the social butterfly. I loved this Jack. I could talk to girls and complete strangers, easily. It was a miracle! I couldn't believe it! All I had to do was drink a lot of this stuff very fast, and I became the person I wanted to be. I grabbed onto this opportunity with both hands and didn't let go. It truly was a social lubricant and a therapist all in one. It was wonderful!

Pot didn't seem to have the same effect on me. I smoked it when it was around, but alcohol was more easily available. Also, I played sports, so I didn't want to hurt my breathing. Hash made everything funny, and all the inanimate boring objects around me suddenly became interesting. It helped in my desperate attempt to find a moment of relief from living afraid.

Sammy took me to many parties where he would abandon me as soon as we got to the door because I would cling to his side. In a twisted way, this mean friend helped me to socialize. I was very competitive, so I saw Sammy as a challenge. If I could outsmart him, then I would be wiser. I set out to conquer my social anxiety through Sammy. I learned how to white-knuckle social situations through hurling myself into Sammy's world.

In the meantime, I was also attending church regularly. I still had to go. I hated church. I liked the people I met at drunken parties much more. Maybe they weren't warm and fuzzy, but at least this competitive world I trusted. I knew you had to be strong to survive.

Church was extremely pretentious. My peers would be very cruel to each other, yet it was in a very nice way. There was a lot of competitiveness, yet it seemed as if everyone insisted this wasn't the case. It was a place to be good in a hateful way. There was the typical struggle for popularity, yet it was a bizarre posturing of who was the nicest. My church peers would be eaten alive in the circles I ran in. They were too naive and weak.

I didn't have a chance in the church world. I was too raw and honest to play the game. My raw honesty was more acceptable in the non-church circles. I felt closer to the libertine crowds because it was familiar to me. I trusted the libertine more. I knew what to expect and it felt real to me. The "dog eat dog" I trusted more than the "nasty nice" social circles.

Also I just hated the church because it was full of people who were pretending to be good when I knew better. They pretended to be perfect. Perfect is impossible. They were self-deluded liars in my mind, very dangerous because they were more unpredictable.

On one of my many sleepless nights, wandering the streets of the city alone, I had a moment of clarity. I decided I was going to find what "it" was all about. I desperately wanted to make an impact in the world by doing something meaningful with my life. I decided to set out and find the meaning and purpose to everything. I wanted to max out all of my potential.

I had always held honesty and truth with reverence. I started to challenge all of my beliefs to see if they would hold water. This was the beginning of a life-or-death journey of discovery. Life needed to make sense to me. I was desperate for understanding. I was oversexed, the violence continued at home, and church felt like the DMV ... boring!

Chapter 4—Middle-School Mayhem

Junior high school was rough. I changed schools again when I moved to junior high school. It was no longer crowds of kids who would attack me. It was always a single bully. I hated bullies. Most of my fights started from trying to protect a weak person from a thug. I was in the learning disabled classes, so I had plenty of chances to rescue people.

The boys I fought were always bigger than me because they were bullies. I was 185 pounds in junior high school, but I was chubby. I was not a lean, mean fighting machine.

I hated bullies, so I would never allow them to operate freely without taking them on. I had huge feelings of helplessness from being abused by the beast, so I felt I had a certain degree of control taking on these smaller opponents. I couldn't take down the beast, so they were the next best thing. It was terrifying, but I couldn't help it. I was an assertive kid. I knew it was righteous.

I got suspended six times in two years in junior high for fighting, and those are the ones where I was caught. The school had a rule; it didn't matter who was at fault, both kids got suspended. I guess they saw it as a cooling-off period.

Of course, I was eligible to play football in eighth grade. I immediately tried out for the team because this is what a warrior would do. I never viewed football as a sport. I saw myself as a gladiator. I never liked sports. I loved being a warrior.

Again, I was a minority, just like in Texas. I was one of a few white kids on the team, yet we were feared and were an excellent team. They had been undefeated for several years straight. I was scared of the huge kids, yet I was going to prove myself strong.

Day after day I endured a physical pounding from these huge inner-city kids. I fought hard and didn't give up. I was getting stronger. They were trying to make me quit the team by breaking me.

The first year I sat the bench, although at this school being second string meant you still got a lot of playing time. We would crush other teams, and so the first string would sit out while they let the rest of us play. The second year, I won a place on the starting team. I didn't get into one fight my ninth grade year. I had built a reputation for myself. I guess I just stayed in one place long enough to do that. I played the tackle position. We remained undefeated until I left for high school.

Most of my fighting stopped after eighth grade. I had grown a few inches and lost my baby fat between eighth and ninth grade. I loved playing for this football team. It was quite prestigious. I was still considered small at 195 pounds, but I was scrappy.

Neither of my parents had anything to do with my playing football. I had no support from them at all. I didn't even expect any support. This is the way the world was to me. I was on my own.

At this time, I was trying to stay away from home as much as possible. Many times I would be startled by a loud crash in the house, followed by my mother screaming for her life and my father beating her down. I hated him. I lived in the basement. Many times I stood on those stairs, completely confused as to what to do, with a loaded shotgun in my hand and the desire to kill the beast in my heart. I desperately wanted him gone.

I wasn't being physically abused by him at this point. He didn't need to. I was terrified of him. I did what he said. He had established that he would use violence from the time I was born. He would intimidate me into obedience. He made sure we didn't ever cross him. He always carried a gun and bragged about his many violent fights or the time he tried to kill a landlord. I believed he would kill me if I gave him a good enough reason.

One time my father made the front of the local newspaper. I was staying at one of my friends' home for a week or so, trying to avoid my house. One morning my friends' mother asked me if I was doing okay. I thought it odd that she was talking to me, because we never talked. Her gaze stayed on me for an uncomfortable few seconds. I said I was great, not knowing why she was so intense. She asked, again, never looking away from me. Again, I said I was fine. Then she finally left me alone. It made me uncomfortable and curious as to why she was all the sudden interested in me. I hated drawing any attention to myself. This couldn't be good.

Later I was told that my father had gone into another tirade and held my mother hostage in the home with a gun. This was nothing new, except that I was very ashamed that people would know. Dad had shot a gun off in the house to bring Mom and us kids into submission before, so that was nothing new. Making the newspaper ... that was new!

As I moved into high school, I had very few friends. I think people knew me, but I only hung out with a handful of guys. Football gave me something to identify with. It gave me a home in the social realms. I was living between private school parties with Sammy and the parties at my school.

I didn't know anyone, but I could tell people had respect for the fact that I played for this football team. My high school had a well-known reputation for being the best football team in the state. Our team won the state championship every two years.

As a freshman, I started the varsity team at defensive tackle. This was very unusual, so I was very proud. I never missed a practice and I fought very hard. I was extremely disciplined. I channeled all my rage and helplessness onto the field. It was the only place that I could allow myself to vent the bottomless pit of rage I had in my belly.

I earned my varsity letter and wore it proudly everywhere I went. I didn't have any money, so it was good that I was a jock. I could get away with wearing sweats and tennis shoes all the time. I believe I would have been bigger if I had eaten well. The biggest I got was 210 pounds. I was always hungry because the house was always empty of food. Being hungry was just a way of life.

At this point a job was not even possible. I did work a job here and there, but I would only be able to work for a few weeks before I was too exhausted to continue. I needed sleep.

Every chance I got, I was looking for sleep. I would sleep sometimes fifteen to eighteen hours at a time. I just couldn't get out of bed. I didn't understand it. It was humiliating.

My dad would continue to say to me that I was "worthless" and "I would never amount to a hill of beans." He called me a "bum" and a "loser." I guess a large part of me believed him because I had always struggled with being tired since I could remember.

When I was in first grade, my mother would splash cold water on my face to wake me up in the mornings. It never worked. Much of the time I went around like a zombie. I hated how tired I was. I was so ashamed that I couldn't beat this tiredness.

Both my sisters and George believed what Dad was saying about me. They were quick to remind me how lazy I was and that I was a bum. I hated them for saying it, but I couldn't argue with the fact that sleep dominated my life.

I had to plan my schedule carefully. What I ended up sacrificing was school. I missed a lot of class. I had to sleep.

An automated call would ring my house when I missed classes. My father knew something was up, so he would sometimes look for me. I would hide in a closet somewhere in the house with a blanket over me and sleep all day. It was terrifying when I would wake up to hear my father's heavy footsteps come in the house. I could tell he was searching for me. He would even open the closet door where I was and peer in. I would hold my breath, panic stricken, until he finally gave up and went back to work. He never found me.

For football, I had to get a weekly eligibility card signed by my teachers to be able to play in the games. I would forge my teachers' signatures so I could play. I missed enough school each year to receive a "no credit" for the year. This meant I had missed so much school that I failed completely.

I became quite masterful at filling out the paperwork to explain each and every day I had missed. I had forged notes and signatures from my parents explaining every absence. I managed to squeak by each year with a D minus average. I only missed one football practice from eighth grade to twelfth grade. I would sleep through school and go to practice.

I was an easy student for teachers. I was actually quite nice. I was never a troublemaker, and I believe this is how I managed to graduate high school. I was a good kid. I would binge drink and get trashed twice a week. I never did homework because I just didn't have the strength emotionally.

I did like literature class. I enjoyed reading short stories and trying to figure out the meaning of each story. The darker the tale, the more I could relate to it. I liked art class as well. I felt I could express my vision of the world to others with paintings and drawings. I would paint pictures of death and rage. I liked drawing skulls, weapons, and violent scenarios where good was overcoming evil. I had constant scenarios running through my mind where I would brutally take out some evil-doer in a most medieval way. I saw myself as a good warrior sacrificing himself for the freedom of others.

I drank heavily. A few times I got alcohol poisoning or blacked out. For the most part, I never got hangovers, though. Drinking was great. I didn't really get any consequences from pounding alcohol, although I started drinking only hard liquor because I had to drink too much liquid to get hammered by beer.

I listened to heavy metal because it was mostly about being bullied by the system and being a slave. I could relate to Metallica's *and Justice for all* or *Master of Puppets* albums or *Countdown to Extinction* by

Megadeath. Anything that had to do with being victimized or enslaved, I could relate too. I also loved Pink Floyd's *The Wall* album. This album spoke to the chaos and hopelessness I was living in.

Everything seemed like a big silly game. Life was surreal to me. With the massive amount of hurt and rage I was dealing with, most of life seemed trivial. I had no Internet at this time, and so my raging lust was channeled through sexual fantasy, fueled by random porn magazines I found. The lust was a raging underground wildfire burning through my life, threatening to overwhelm my above-ground life at any time. As awkward as I was, I started to talk to girls because it was fun.

I would usually fall hopelessly in love with a girl from a distance. The girl I fell in love with, I would never think about sexually. I knew my lust was bad and out of control, so I only thought sexually about girls I didn't love. This was my reasoning as I started to approach girls.

The girls I approached mostly were other poor souls who were starved for attention. I begrudgingly followed my lust into situations where I would be physical with a girl, and then later I would feel terrible because this was not what, I believed, a good warrior should do. Despite my noble beliefs about women, the lust was showing itself too strong for me to control. The struggle between wanting to be a hero and rescue a girl was being challenged by my heart, which was a love-starved black hole threatening to destroy everything in my life. My lust was unreasonable and exacted a huge toll from my energy. It was humiliating to be ruled by this starving entity. Fortunately for me I met a girl whom I loved, and she loved me back in her own quirky way.

Chapter 5—Crazy Love

My mother was always trying to become famous in some way or another. She was very beautiful. She wanted to be a famous singer the most. She had visions of grandeur for herself. She was always finding a way to perform in front of crowds. One particular performance was held at a community center in rural Virginia.

I came to that performance the summer after my eleventh grade year. As I first stepped through the front door, I saw a beautiful skinny blonde girl rushing through the main entrance hall. I was smitten. She looked foreign.

Later I saw her in the show. She was one of the girls modeling clothes for the local stores. I was not going to leave that night without introducing myself to her. At intermission, I went down to the green room and introduced myself to her. I was shocked that she was so beautiful and she was actually talking to me.

After the show was over that night, I met her for a few moments again and got her phone number. I wrote it on the back of the ticket stub from that night, and I still have that ticket to this day. We lived an hour apart and neither of us was able to drive, so a phone grew out of my ear that summer. We talked for hours at a time. Our relationship was instant magnetism.

As I got to know her, I found that she was a bit socially awkward. Her emotions were unpredictable as well. She didn't take real good care of herself because her clothes were usually disheveled and her hair was a mess. She had way too much makeup and a child's sense of humor. She was very unpredictable in the company of others. She would have sudden random outbursts of laughing; other times it would be rage. She was so cute, though, and I could tell that she was harmless. She mostly was her own worst enemy.

I could also tell, right away, that she was quite vulnerable, because she had no idea how beautiful she really was. It was as though her beauty didn't exist. This told me she had some serious self-confidence problems. My mission became to help this girl recognize how beautiful she was so she would not be so vulnerable to bad people who wanted to take advantage of her. She was naïve, and this was very bad for a girl who was so beautiful. She was my princess to rescue.

She was perfect for me. I fell deeply in love with her, and she was so beautiful that she could do no wrong in my eyes. I started dating her exclusively.

I wanted to keep her so badly that I lied to her about my partying lifestyle. I came across as a person who didn't drink. I also didn't try to get her to have sex with me because she was a girl I loved, and this should be her decision. I wanted to win her affection by overwhelming her with poetry, love letters, and chivalry. I tried to keep out of control, lazy-bum "Jack" hidden, because she represented hope to me. I desperately wanted to overcome what I thought were bad character traits and be her knight in shining armor.

Angelica and I stayed together. She was extremely loyal, very naïve, and had a lot of rage she carried with her. She was atypical. Angelica was a neglected little girl raised in a family where money was regarded as *the* life-giving agent.

She was a hard worker. A job alone was the single most important endeavor there was in life, according to her father. Angelica was not a fully developed person; she was very one-dimensional because of these values. Her life was lacking peace and fullness. Job was king; anything else was a worthless pursuit, insubstantial. Angelica was a little girl who was taught to hold onto work with both hands and never let go or she would fall to her doom.

This made her unpredictable and hostile in social situations. She was very defensive and fearful because she didn't know how to protect herself. She was very awkward, yet had no reservations about this. She was all or nothing in her approach to life, and I admired her tenacity. She was impossible to reason with, but I just saw this as a challenge. I was going to win her over.

Chapter 6—Jousting Windmills

As my senior year approached, I had made up my mind to go to college. I just wanted to play football. Football had given me a place in the social circles. I loved the brutality of football and that I was able to access the rage inside and channel it into something substantial for myself. Football became my purpose in life.

I had no other choice. The military was appealing, but at this point I was too terrified of authority and being controlled. It was terrifying to think of joining the military because I had already been ruined when it came to trusting anything.

In the circles I ran in, it was just a natural progression to go to college. It was expected of everyone. I was extremely disciplined at this point. I was good at working my life around sleeping ten to eighteen hours at a time. Football became my one and only goal in life. I believed that if I worked hard enough, anything was possible.

I did things in a big way, and I was a man of my word, so when I set my sights on the NFL, it was going to happen. I believed I could will it to happen. Football was the only thing I was good at and consistent with. It was my lifeline to doing something meaningful in a world that was hostile.

I was told by coaches that I wasn't big enough or fast enough to play in the NFL. I trusted no one, and I didn't believe anyone had my best interest at heart. Unfortunately, I was forced to make decisions in a vacuum. I had tunnel vision, and I could only trust myself. On this lonely mountain top, I had to make a blind decision about my life with absolutely no guidance at all. I knew I wasn't a great football player. I was good, but not great.

I was going to be like Conan the Barbarian and forge my destiny through blood and sweat. I just saw the NFL as "all the odds were against me." I fought my way onto the great teams I played on in the past ... It didn't seem so crazy that I could do this again with college and then the NFL. I had overcome impossible odds with football before and won. It's all I knew.

I had a tremendous amount of self-hatred and disgust at this point, and so I also saw it as somehow redeeming myself to a world that was telling me I was a loser, a bum, and that I would never amount to anything. I wanted to prove them all wrong. I had zero guidance, so, unfortunately, I picked an impossible goal.

I got a scholarship to a college, yet I ignored it because it wasn't Division 1. I traveled around to a couple schools accompanied by a friend or by myself. I only went to Division 1 schools. When I got there, I saw that most of the players were much stronger and faster than me, and it was because of weightlifting. I set out to conquer weightlifting. This was going to be my ticket to play.

I was very idealistic. Steroids were not an option, because I had a strong will. It was too late by the time I realized that steroids was the only way I could have played Division 1 ball. I was "a day late and a dollar short" to most things because I was completely alone with no guidance.

That summer after my senior year, I went to live with Angelica at her house. I never ate so well. I gained fifty pounds in a couple months. I only saw it as fat, though, so I humiliated myself enough to starve it off. I was used to being hungry, so it was nothing new to me. I started weightlifting religiously and starving myself. I need to be muscular, strong, and fast with no extra, useless weight.

I didn't realize at the time that my body was becoming what it should have been in normal circumstances. If I had eaten regularly in high school, I would have been much bigger. I would have been better at football too. I was always hungry. Hunger was a way of life for me; it was a part of the landscape.

I tried to make it on the team of a couple Division 1 schools. I went to try-outs and got rejected every time. I had no money to go to college and the fall classes were starting in a couple of weeks. I desperately wanted to play college football.

My brother, George, and my sister, Nellie, stopped to see me on the way to the college they were currently attending. I was in a miserable situation. I explained to George that I was here at this school with no money to attend.

My parents had dropped me off a week earlier, but my dad gave me $20 and I sent them home telling them it would work out. I had hoped to get a walk-on scholarship. My dad walked away from me when he realized I needed help. He turned away from me, walked back to the car, and drove off. Mother ignored my distress and followed after Dad.

George drove me to his school, King College, where he helped me get in the door. I got anonymous financial help from some church members at the local church. I was able to get college loans, and I was on academic probation until I could prove I could make the grades needed.

I did not want to go to King College because there was no football team. My plan was to use the time there to get stronger on the weights, then transfer out ASAP to a football school.

I could see that the competition was over my head, so I dedicated my life to the weight room. Each semester after that, I would try to transfer out of King College. I desperately wanted my dream to come true.

As I kept trying to go to another college, something else would come up. I didn't have the funds, it was an out of state school so I couldn't afford it, I only got partial scholarships, or I just didn't file the correct paperwork on time. I was learning everything from scratch. By the time I finally did successfully transfer to play football at a Division 2 school; it was very late in the game. It was my junior year.

Finally I was on a team. When I finally got there, I saw that almost everyone was on steroids. I simply could not compete with that. I was still very determined not to use steroids. I was going to make it with blood, sweat, and tears. Well ... I needed the steroids. By the time I had this realization, I had graduated from King College.

I left football finally after one semester. I transferred back to King College to graduate. I could see I didn't have enough time to play. I had to graduate in one year. There was just no time to play catch-up. The ship had sailed. I was losing myself.

During all of this time, I was still binge drinking. I was catching rides home on the weekends until Angelica went to school about forty-five minutes away. I was struggling with bad heart palpitations and horrible anxiety. I was having recurrent nightmares. In the middle of the night, I would jump out of the bed suddenly and run across the room, only to find myself standing by the window. I was having nightmares about being covered in spiders. Sometimes I would be suffocating and paralyzed, half awake, staring into the dark room, unable to breathe or move, absolutely helpless and terrified.

Chapter 7—Madness

Weightlifting was an obsession. I had managed to get my body fat down to 9 percent. This is very low for someone with a body type like mine. Each time I ran into another roadblock, I would punish myself with weightlifting and starvation. I hated myself for being weak and fat. Fat was the enemy. Like a Spartan, I used these workouts and starvation to make me stronger. I would punish my body to make it overcome weakness. I was miserable, but I had a six pack. I was trying to prove to the world I wasn't lazy and worthless. I kept myself at 9 percent body fat for years.

It was also a simple issue of survival. I felt that I had to work out. I had no choice. I had to keep myself strong at all times or else I could be preyed upon. It is a dog-eat-dog world, and I have Milk-Bone underwear on. Fighting is life.

I pursued a journalism degree. I picked journalism because it was easy for me and I had a friend that was going into it also. I enjoyed creative writing class where I got to vent my frustrations with the world. Literature classes and creative writing gave me an opportunity to try to make sense of the world. I stopped believing in God. I was agnostic in my worldview.

I enjoyed American Literature where we studied the Transcendentalists: Emerson, Thoreau, and Walt Whitman. I was completely intrigued by their search to make sense of the world around them. They brought up real existential issues that I, myself, struggled with. There was no meaning to life in my world. I found the power of venting my fears and frustrations in a journal. Journaling became my way of trying to make sense of the world.

As my dreams became shattered, I drifted deeper into a nihilistic worldview where everything is nothing. A dark chasm of meaninglessness and hopelessness was opening under me, pulling me into a terrifying hell. I was slipping, losing my sanity and connection with the world around me. My life was becoming a horror show. The darkness in my life was growing at a much faster rate, and the light was being snuffed out.

I raged against God when I thought he might be there. Other times I would huddle on a cold, dark ledge overlooking a giant meaningless void that I envisioned life to be. Then it got worse.

After I graduated school, I went to live with Angelica while she finished her degree. She still had two years to go. During the summer, I found a book on child abuse. As I read the pages, I realized that I was being profiled. As the realization dawned on me that I was abused, the damn broke that held what was left of my sanity in place. I read and studied the whole book. Yep ... I was abused. All the signs were there. This was absolutely devastating to me because I realized that I was broken, and that's the way I would always be. I did everything the book told me to. The last part of the book said to confront your abuser if it is safe to do so. I believed my dad would kill me, so I let it go.

The previous summer my dad had words with me. He wanted to fight me. I was minding my own business when he walked up in front of me and began to take off his rings. It had been years since I knocked him out in the street. It was still eating at him. I wasn't real surprised, but I was scared. I hated fighting with him. I just told him that I didn't want to fight him. He finally left me alone. I was afraid he would kill me with a gun.

Internet porn was on the scene by this time. I was addicted to pornography; I couldn't work for any extended period of time, and I was struggling to find a reason to not kill myself. Suicide came to occupy my mind frequently.

I believed I was the problem in my relationship with Angelica. I was angry at myself for not having the courage to commit suicide and release this loyal girl from me. I hated myself and saw myself as garbage. I was a failure with my dreams shattered.

During this time, I boxed in the Golden Gloves. I had a fleeting hope that I could be a pro boxer. I was too late in the game for that one also. The guys who did well were trained from when they were young. I knocked guys out and I got knocked out. I won some and I lost some. I was tough, but I just wasn't good enough to make a career out of it.

My anxiety attacks continued. I was sleeping more than ever now, and I was up all night and slept all day. I was seriously dissociating from the world around me. Life was very surreal. I couldn't tell the difference between dream and reality. I thought maybe I was someone else's nightmare. I would sit in the closet staring off into space for hours at a time with a look of horror on my face.

I took philosophy classes at Angelica's school, where I devoured the books but I failed the class. Sleep and depression were dominating my life. Alcohol had changed its effect on me. I started becoming more reckless each time I drank, more unpredictable. Drinking just made me feel depressed now; it was no longer a high. Life truly was turning out to be meaningless and random. Mankind was born out of a puddle of mud, and I just couldn't live with the idea of being dust, meaningless particles, random.

I lay in bed all of the time. I never wanted to come out from under the sheets. I was going from a super high adrenaline charge to crashing and burning. The crashing and burning was becoming more and more frequent. I was getting into fights again on the street or in the apartment complex where Angelica lived. I was beating guys up pretty bad for being all-around a nuisance to society. I went to court and won because I was a good guy. I beat down bullies when I found them.

Of all my studying, Saint Augustine appealed to me the most. Many of the philosophers I read would talk about how to reach or "transcend" your current situation. Any kind of idealistic, optimistic fairytale about overcoming my shattered self was not on the table for me. I could tell I was ruined; beyond repair.

In Saint Augustine's "confessions," he opened each entry by saying what a miserable creature he was. He saw himself as hopeless but for the Grace of God. I could relate to his demoralized state.

I found it odd that I was relating to a Christian at this point, because I would not even wear a cross around my neck. Augustine saw man as depraved, and I could not ignore that reality. I could see that I was truly a limited organism, debased.

My life was riddled with self-disgust, self-hatred, and crushing shame. I wanted to kill myself, yet I felt a responsibility to somehow find a way; a responsibility to Angelica. I loved her tremendously and killing myself would have deeply scarred her. For some unorthodox reason, Angelica was highly loyal to me.

A part of me was hoping she would leave me so I could no longer ruin her life. I wanted her to fall out of love for me so I could go, be miserable, and die alone, not harming anyone. She was still there, so I believed I had to make this right. I felt horribly selfish because I didn't have the courage to walk away from her for her sake.

Chapter 8—Just A Rat

I was lost. I worked out religiously even at this time. Everything I had ever earned up to this point that felt like any value had to do with my physical strength. I also had a fear of being overpowered or killed. The only thing that was real to me at this time was that the world was an extremely hostile place and that I had to stay strong to survive. Working out and staying fit was an absolute necessity to me. I could see the underbelly of the American culture. I knew things could fly apart at any moment and that everyone would be more interested in self-preservation. This is the world I grew up in.

The people who are not dangerous get ruled by the people who are dangerous. Any talk of goodness, love, charity, and a good God was just another angle weaker people used when they wanted power and control. If someone really did buy into these values, I considered them weak and easily manipulated by the cruel. Violence ruled the world. I lived this reality, and I couldn't be convinced otherwise. So I punished my body to stay strong.

At this time I was a drifter of sorts. I had no job because my body had a mind of its own. Like a raw nerve, I was hopelessly exposed to the indiscriminate whims of my emotional state. My life was arbitrary. I was a slave to some greater force that I had no control over whatsoever. I was humiliated and demoralized. I saw myself as a slave with absolutely no power to change my destiny. The helplessness fueled my despair. Something had to give eventually; I didn't know what, but I couldn't continue like this without some kind of consequence. My body finally cracked.

The crushing anxiety and extreme fatigue manifested itself as chronic urinary pain. I just woke up one day with the symptoms of a urinary tract infection. I was devastated when the expert doctors I went to see just had no clue how to help me. They couldn't explain it. There was no bacterium, yet I had all the signs of a urinary infection. I was a medical mystery to John Hopkins Hospital. It was finally concluded that it must be psychologically related.

This chronic condition came up when I had just found a contact to buy steroids. I had researched the different types of steroids and how best to administer them. I was going to inject them with a needle so as to bypass the kidneys; this was considered a bit safer.

I had chosen Deca Durabolin or "D-ball," because it promised the best results. I was going to do steroids finally, and with my newfound size and strength, try to get into the NFL. It was my last-ditch effort.

At this point I had come to learn how dramatic the effects of steroids were when it came to athletic prowess. With D-ball, I could gain twenty pounds of muscle in six weeks and increase my squat and max bench press exponentially. I saw what steroids could do. They truly are a magic pill.

After my affliction showed up, though, my only interest became getting better. I dropped my drug contact because I knew steroids would only complicate this mystery. Steroids were already an enigma and the added mystery affliction would just make it an enigma within an enigma.

My dream was shattered, and I had it replaced with a chronic affliction. My outlook was grim, and it looked like my dad was right about me. I was a worthless loser who would never amount to anything. My life had become a horror show. I was devastated. If I hadn't had Angelica, I would have been living with the homeless and would have eventually killed myself. She was my one and only constraint at this time.

The days and nights melded together, one into the next. I was isolated and alone, save Angelica, who had no clue how to help me. I was sleeping for fifteen to twenty hours at a time. My whole life was now a slave to my exhaustion and sleeping. I could come up with no reason to even try at life. I was overpowered by a deep sense of meaninglessness. There was no reason to do anything, because all was a worthless pursuit of self-indulgence, and I did not have the ego strength to get up and try anymore. Why bother? The trouble with winning the rat race is that you are still a rat in the end.

Chapter 9—The Devil Made Me Do It

My sister Sally was always trying to save my soul at this time. She wanted me to turn to Jesus so he would help me. The problem I had with Sally is that I could see no happiness in her life. She was neurotic about religion and this, to me, was clearly because it wasn't working. She had no peace.

We would argue about proof of the existence of God. She would not stay intellectually honest when we argued. She would blindly hold onto beliefs with no reflection at all. I wasn't buying what she was selling because she was clearly so unhappy and hostile toward my questions about God.

When Sally could not answer a question I had, she would show contempt for me and say that I was being antagonistic. Sally saw any kind of questioning God as disobedience. I was asking sincere questions and she would get defensive and accuse me of being a troublemaker. I could see she was using this strategy to cover for her ignorance. She was blindly following an ideology and she called this faith. This was not faith, this was fear.

My brother George would also attempt to reach me with religion, and he was doing the same thing as Sally. George would grow impatient with my constant questions and write me off as antagonistic. This really hurt my feelings. I was sincere. George and Sally both would look at me with contempt, and this was not going to win me over to their god. They were both very arrogant and were only interested in winning. I wasn't born yesterday; they were only interested in being right and not understanding me.

After years of this kind of treatment, George actually said three little words that got my attention. It was the first Thanksgiving after Angelica had graduated from college. Angelica and I were staying at the apartment until the lease ran out. I was home visiting on Thanksgiving.

George started into me about God. I held my ground as usual with intellectual honesty. I asked a few very tough questions about God and George, for the first time, said "I don't know." This grabbed my attention because George had heard my question and was honest. This intrigued me.

George told me about this church he was going to in Texas. He invited me to come join him there and go to this church. He had confidence in the pastor to help answer my difficult questions.

It was never a question for me as to whether or not I would go. This is the first time someone had taken me seriously and promised me to get my questions answered, although something quite bizarre happened that night.

My mind was an asylum filled with parasitical life-stealing worms. My heart was still beating, but decay was taking hold. Life was a kaleidoscope of nightmares. I could only see broken shards and nothing was whole. Each shard was suicide, despair, brokenness, and darkness—a collage of horrors. I knew this could not last.

After seeing that George had said something intellectually honest, I moved in the direction of researching the "God" idea. George asked me to get down on my knees and pray. I decided to go through the motions as an academic exercise. In that moment, my mouth said, "No!" My body immediately leaped backwards and sat on the couch.

I was somewhat taken back by this. I didn't feel any different, but my body clearly didn't want to kneel. I got up off the couch and was able to kneel and pray the second time. I was confused, but I was not afraid at all.

George was more afraid than I. He got the pastor from Texas on the phone and he labeled the experience as demonic. If it were demonic, I had lived with this thing, and so I wasn't afraid. I was actually hoping it was demonic, because the pastor said he could throw out the demons that I had. I was very skeptical, yet hopeful this could work. I wasn't totally buying it, but I really had nowhere else to go. I was completely alone with no guidance: desperate.

I decided to give God another chance, even though it seemed a horrible exercise in redundancy. I had been down this road and I hated that place. I was escaping the burning home that was my life, so I struck out in the direction of faeries, goblins, and ghosts, where people were too scared to see the reality of the dark precipice that humanity was teetering on. I saw religion as Karl Marx put it: "The opium of the masses," but when you are drowning, you will claw for anything to stay afloat.

I decided to give God six months of my life. That was the deal. I would go to this church in Texas and see what would happen, but I would abandon this path if it produced nothing. I was extremely skeptical, to say the least. Angelica had just graduated with her college degree and so we moved to Texas together.

Chapter 10—Get Plenty Of Exorcise

Church was really not my scene, and so it was an awkward time. I couldn't relate to people who tried so hard to get along. It was suspicious behavior to me; I didn't trust it.

The church had some rules I needed to follow if I were going to stay. The pastor said I should marry Angelica or let her go now. I had to make a choice. It created a lot of pressure for me to make a decision, and so I picked to marry her. I couldn't imagine myself without her in my life.

In the meantime, Pastor Bill Baker met with me to do an exorcism. There were other strangers there from the church that held staff and lay positions. I didn't know anyone. The pastor wanted to make sure I was humble enough to spend time with and that is why, he explained, he brought in strangers.

The meeting began by the pastor asking anyone if they had unconfessed sins that could interfere with the exorcism. That being done, they would pray for God to guide them and for there to be deliverance.

I was sitting in a chair across from the pastor and everyone else was on my right and left. I noticed some of them looked like they were new to this as well. After praying, the pastor would level his gaze at me and begin to address the demons.

The pastor would address the demons and ask them to give their name and to name the sin that allowed access to me. Like a broken record, this went on for a long time. The pastor would boom his voice in a deep authoritative manor while looking into my face, waiting for a reply.

I was fearful I would somehow interrupt the progress because I believed at this time I was very depraved and unworthy of anything good. I hated myself. I was afraid God would consider me lazy and difficult like my father did. I was terrified I would do something wrong, and I wanted to be as much of a help as I could.

We went on for about twenty minutes with nothing happening, and the pastor got more demanding and aggressive as time went on. I was very disappointed that nothing was happening, and I felt I must be a very difficult person because even Jesus had a hard time getting the demons out of me.

I really wanted it to work, but nothing was happening, and so I grasped for whatever I could think of to fill the silence. I was starving for help, and this was the first time someone had put aside time for me. I didn't want to be labeled disobedient and difficult. Nothing was happening, and I asked what I should do. The pastor told me to just say whatever came to my mind. I did just that.

It was as if I opened the door from a quiet museum out onto a busy New York street. Whatever came to my mind poured out my mouth: sounds, words, memories, were all unceremoniously shoved out my mouth. Gibberish and nonsensical word pictures were vomited out into the air. I was trying really hard to help. I saw this as being sincere and a hard worker. I figured they could work out the gibberish because they were not particularly surprised by my indiscriminate, nonspecific, yet animated exhibition.

Finally, after a few hours of this, Pastor Bill Baker wrapped up the meeting. He seemed quite satisfied with the progress. I was disappointed because I was hoping for a dramatic delivery from the horrible pain and depression I was under. I was still hopelessly depressed, and now I was physically exhausted after being yelled at for a few hours. The pastor was optimistic, but I was more confused and felt like this was a hopeless pursuit. I felt as if my problems were much too big for God or that God just didn't care. I was hopeful I could be delivered, but it wasn't going to happen that night.

Another requirement for me to attend the church was that I needed to have a mentor. An assistant pastor and his wife stepped in to help us. Bobby and Helen Jennings continued the demonic sessions the pastor had started with me. I would go to these demonic sessions with Bobby Jennings twice a week for three years. Each session could last up to three to four hours.

I kept reaching into my Rolodex of despair and shame in my mind to access more demons. Bobby Jennings was quite satisfied with the progress. I would come up with shameful things I had done in the past and attach a name to it. This was called a demon and Bobby would then "bring it before the throne of Christ" and cast it out.

I was always disappointed with each session. I never felt better afterwards. I would tell my wife I didn't believe it was working, but we didn't know of anything else to do. Assistant Pastor Bobby Jennings would relentlessly hammer away, throwing out demon after demon, and I went along with it because I was desperate to get better.

I constantly struggled with suicide and discouragement. The sessions were not working. I did everything I was told, but my shame was too much for me to be able to stand my ground and tell them it wasn't working and quit. I didn't want to believe I was hopeless, so I kept going to the exorcisms. I blamed myself for everything; it had to be my fault that I wasn't being healed. I kept going because I had nowhere else to go.

Bobby Jennings started a recovery program. I began going to it and it was a good place for me, at first. I would go to the groups and be honest about my struggles with others. It was the first place where I could share my struggles in public. For a few months Bobby would hint that he wanted me to become a small group leader. I wanted nothing to do with leading; I felt I was in no shape to do such a thing.

I continued to attend, but I could tell my mentor was not happy about this. Finally, the dreadful happened; I had no intention of leading and I wanted nothing to do with it, but Bobby finally told me I had to lead. The moment he told me this, I went into a panic attack and mental breakdown; the responsibility was too much. He rushed me into the church and started an exorcism on me right away.

I couldn't say no to this man. He had put a lot of time and effort toward me, and it was time to cash in. While terrified of the responsibility, I told him I would lead. Assistant Pastor Bobby Jennings had bought me through, leveraging his time spent with me. I felt too guilty to say no. I had to do it because I felt it was the honorable thing to do because he had sacrificed so much for me. It was awful.

I became a leader in the recovery program. I was in recovery for six years of my life. Recovery was good because it got me around other people who wanted to better themselves. I never found full recovery, though, because I was forced to lead, which killed any chance for healing because the responsibility stole my freedom.

After a few years of leading, I came to my mentor, Bobby Jennings, and told him I wanted to take a break because I was overwhelmed. I was hoping he would give me permission to stop leading. He was incensed that I even asked, and he said that if I quit then I would never be allowed back into the program. I now believe that the recovery program we used was good, but it never worked for me because I never voluntarily went into the program. I was forced to lead, so I had no chance to heal. Bobby Jennings abused his position as assistant pastor when he took advantage of my weakened state.

Chapter 11—Strings Attached

Pastor Bill was big on education. He was a professor at the local seminary; he was a church planter, and a pastor. Bill Baker spent much of his time training small groups to go out into the world and plant churches.

I went to Bill for help on difficult existential questions. He pointed me in the direction of some amazing books that helped me to see there were legitimate, sincere, and intelligent people who held a Christian worldview. I read books like *The Universe Next Door*, by James Sire, and *The God Who is There*, by Francis Schaefer. These authors, along with Bill Baker's teaching of the Bible, led me to believe that it was very likely there is a God.

I started to see that the Bible did apply to everyday life situations. The first book of the Bible I read was Ecclesiastes. I was shocked when the author of Ecclesiastes was saying that life was purposeless and without meaning; I could relate to this. The Bible addresses human suffering and has some intriguing explanations as to why I even exist.

Bill Baker was excellent at using the Bible to explain modern problems. He made the Bible real to me. Bill used much of the Old Testament to explain that there are moral laws at work in the world, and if you do not respect them, then this brings much hardship and trouble into your life. I was very relieved to see that there are reliable patterns in the world; it isn't all just meaningless chaos.

I immersed myself into Bill Baker's teachings and the Bible. I was excited to see so many explanations about the world around me. I had to meet some conditions if I were to join Bill Baker's church. These conditions were a way for Pastor Bill to assure I was going to follow the rules of his church.

The first condition was that I should marry Angelica right away. I had to make a choice immediately to either marry her or break up with her. This was a very painful decision for me because I was so hopelessly fearful of being alone that I couldn't bring myself to make a rational decision at this point. I picked to marry her even though I felt it was horribly selfish. I knew I was a mess and that I was ruining her life. The marriage day was extremely stressful, and I did everything to keep a smile on my face that day.

The other conditions all had to do with serving. I had to serve in nursery once a month, and I had to attend church regularly or my church membership would be revoked. I signed a contract when I joined to guarantee I would be available to serve. Bill reiterated serving over and over again. Serving was the way to make yourself acceptable to the leadership and get kudos from your peers.

Bill made it very clear that in order to be acceptable, you had to make yourself useful; otherwise you were worthless and of no value to the church. The only way to prove to God that you love him was to serve, action. There was a quiet understanding that prevailed with all of the church members that one was either useful or useless.

I was desperately distressed by the requirement to serve. I was serving in the recovery program twice a week, serving in the preschool on Sunday mornings, I never missed church on Sunday, I attended home fellowship during the week, and I had nursery duty once a month. I went to every meeting and retreat, and I went to every seminar that was held. It was silently understood by all that one must be on call at all times or your loyalty and character came into question.

I constantly felt a nagging sense of inadequacy under these expectations. There were others who were much better than me at serving, and they got honored in front of the church by a mention from the pastor. I knew I would never be good enough to be honored, but I could at least try and keep myself from being kicked out and publicly humiliated by the pastor. That is where I set the bar so I wouldn't get called out. Pastor Bill had openly rebuked others in the past, and he wasn't afraid to do it again.

Over time, my resentment and contempt for the pastor grew. I received a lot of good help from him in understanding how the world works according to the Bible, yet he was also burdening me tremendously with serving. I didn't want to resent him, but he made this impossible for me. Over time as the years went by, like a noose slowly tightening around my neck, the pressure from performing grew. I hated this; I wanted to like the pastor.

I was learning a tremendous amount about how the Bible applies to life, yet I was still wounded and tired. I was becoming more and more discouraged because I thought serving was supposed to bring life at some point. I had a pretty solid biblical worldview, yet I was exhausted and still wanted to commit suicide after eleven years of attending Bill Baker's church and six years of a recovery program.

Chapter 12—None the Wiser

I was exasperated, afraid of being publicly rebuked by the pastor, and suicidal. I saw God as good yet unyielding. I bought into the notion that I was a worm and the only thing that made me good was the fact that God saved my pathetic self. I had to prove to God that I loved him through doing good.

I believed I was saved and going to heaven no matter what I did, but this only tempted me even more to want to kill myself. I wanted to escape the tremendous shame that was eating away at my soul. I constantly felt like a huge disappointment to God because I still couldn't keep a full-time job and I couldn't seem to beat the feelings of hopelessness and despair that strangled me.

I wasn't able to work a full-time job. This was a tremendous, bitter, shame for me at a church where a man was measured by his ability to overcome his weak nature and endure hardship. Men were encouraged to "buck up" and always pick the most difficult path. I constantly felt emasculated in the presence of any man who could keep a full-time job so his wife didn't need to work.

I did everything I was told by Bill Baker, and I still could not seem to gain momentum in my life. After eleven years, panic was setting in. I had absorbed all of Bill Baker's teachings and I was still miserable. I gained a great education; I even got a master's degree in counseling psychology at the local seminary during that time. I wanted life when I moved to Texas, but instead I got an education. I was chasing the proverbial "carrot on a stick." I was told I would find life through serving others, and after eleven years of serving, I was still miserable and dead inside.

I was still working part time, and I couldn't handle the pressure of working a full-time job. I believed God must hate me because I was worthless and useless. I tried my best, but I was quite unimpressive by the Christian world's standards. I saw myself as a huge weakling among men. Not being able to handle much pressure, and my wife supporting me financially, was an unforgivable crime in this Christian community.

I struggled with a particular verse. The verse was Jesus speaking, and he said, "My yoke is easy and my burden is light." I couldn't understand how this verse applied in a world where men were supposed to white-knuckle difficulty all the time. My pastor had assured me that nothing worthwhile ever came easily for a man. Easy was for wimps, according to Bill Baker.

I still felt very insignificant and small in the universe. I saw life as a struggle between God and the Devil, and I was a pawn in their power struggle. I had learned I was completely powerless and worthless on my own, and if it wasn't for the grace of Jesus then I would be in hell also. Sure, Jesus and God are good, but they were not healing me, so that could only reinforce what my father told me—I am "a lazy bum who will never amount to anything." I was saved, but I was useless to everyone including God.

Chapter 13—Suffocating

After eleven years at Bill Baker's church, I felt compelled to leave. Bill Baker had an insatiable appetite when it came to gleaning every bit of service he could out of an individual. Pastor Bill's ideology on serving was a black hole that sucked the very marrow of life out of my spirit. I was burned out and desperate for change, burdened beyond belief.

Another force I couldn't explain drove me to move from Texas back to northern Virginia. My body was defying my mind. I was trying very hard to make a decision as to whether I would move or not while my body already had its mind made up. I was suffocating in Pastor Bill's church, and, like a drowning person, I swam for the surface for air.

I was very scared to make the transition because I was told that if I didn't have the accountability of the church community, I would surely fall into a horribly depraved and destructive lifestyle. I was told that the Devil would single me out from the flock and take me down. Regardless, I drove away from Dallas in an exasperated, life-starved fury.

I knew the next major challenge in my life was going to be my and Angelica's families. We were moving back to where our parents and siblings lived. We only saw them on holidays, but now we were going to be in their lives on a regular basis.

I had been researching how to become a high school teacher in Virginia since right before we left Dallas. I was hoping that, this time, I could get a full-time job and that by some miracle I would keep it. I had been working for the Dallas independent school district as a substitute teacher for several years, so it seemed feasible.

I was still holding on to the seemingly impossible scenario of me working full time and Angelica not having to work at all. Angelica got a job as an accountant at a local church, and I got a job as a substitute teacher for the local school district.

As an act of faith, I decided to try to have a baby with Angelica. I could see that Angelica and I weren't getting any younger, and I didn't want Angelica to have any regrets for herself or resent me for never trying to have a child. I didn't want to be responsible for coming between Angelica and her full potential as a woman. I wasn't going to rob her of having this wonderful experience; I felt I had brought enough trouble into her life already. I wanted to be a part of the solution, not a part of the problem.

I saw myself as on the verge of getting a good job as a teacher. We bought a nice town home in a decent neighborhood. My dream was to fully support my wife so she did not have to work and we could have a family. This had always been my goal. It looked very plausible, despite the deeper, nagging despair of my past failed attempts. I needed to keep hurling myself into this closed door because I was hoping to impress God so He would move to help me.

I knew the black cloud of instability, insomnia, and social anxiety wasn't far behind; nonetheless, I thought God would surely bless me with the strength to achieve these things because they were so close to His heart. God would finally heal me from this affliction where I would crash and burn from exhaustion, anxiety, and depression three months into any full-time job I had ever worked in the past.

I still believed what Pastor Bill Baker taught me ... that if I sacrifice myself as a man for the greater good, God would bless me, but only after I had proven my faith and love in action. I desperately wanted to redeem myself from the stigma of being, in my dads' words, "a lazy, good-for-nothing bum who would never amount to a hill of beans," which is a belief synonymous with Bill Baker's theology. Pastor Bill taught that

all people are selfish, lazy, and foolish, and that they need constant accountability or they will fall into depravity at the first chance they get.

As I was preparing to become a full-time teacher, I was once again
confronted with my inability to follow through. The pressure of the job
was too much for me, and so I had to quit after three and a half years
combined of being a substitute teacher in Texas and Virginia.

Chapter 14—Shock

A year earlier, as I had been looking for places to work, I met a woman by the name of Mary Theresa. She was a chaplain who ran an organization called Care Ministries. In the brief time I spent with her, she had made a strong impression on me.

Chaplain Mary struck me as odd because she had so much enthusiasm. She worked with hospice and specialized in grief and loss. I had never met anyone with so much optimism and faith in Jesus Christ. All the Christians I was used to seeing were very burdened with trying to please Jesus. I never forgot about her, so when my substituting job fell through, I decided to sell our town home and move to Warrenton so I could work under her mentorship.

Chaplain Mary was retirement age, yet each time I spoke to her I was inspired. She had a huge smile and she bubbled with life. She was a mature age, but she had the spirit of a happy child. I wanted what she had. I wanted to be enthusiastic and full of optimism like her, so I went to volunteer at her organization after substitute teaching failed.

I decided to pursue being a licensed counselor for the state of Virginia. I had the master's degree in psychology from Texas, yet Virginia had much stricter guidelines for becoming a counselor, so I would have to take a few more classes and get a lot more internship hours. I did not want to do this, but I thought that this must be what God wanted me to do because He had me meet Chaplain Mary.

Right away I started volunteering as a counselor. I was going to get the internship hours I needed working at Care Ministries. Working under Chaplain Mary, I learned about grief, mourning, and loss. She had an appreciation for the devastating effects of emotional pain, pain that one could not see. I got certified in grief and loss and so began helping those who were in deep pain.

I was good at helping others in the process of healing from their wounds; however, I had the paralyzing affects of the nameless wound I was still bleeding from.

I didn't understand why, but my ability to handle responsibility was not there. I was flooding inside. I was saturated with pain and loss. I could only limp myself through life. Emotionally, my tank was empty. I was running on fumes, and the feelings of helplessness and powerlessness were humiliating me. I was still at a loss.

I had always had an unquenchable thirst to self-improve. I never stopped reading books and seeking answers. I would always be researching to find the answers to my struggles. I came across post-traumatic stress disorder in my research. I read the profile for someone with PTSD, and it read like my diary.

I never spared any expense when it came to anything that might help me, so I immediately found classes and got certified in PTSD. I had never seen anything like it before. I was a worst-case scenario. I had what was called complex PTSD, which meant my trauma was not a one-time event but had happened continuously over a long period of time. The experts were telling me I had brain damage from abuse and that this was a serious, debilitating condition. I was able to finally put a name to my struggle, complex PTSD. I diagnosed myself as having PTSD.

I had always been open to my mentors and leaders about my struggles, so it was natural that I shared the possibility of me having PTSD with Chaplain Mary. Chaplain Mary did something profoundly simple that I had never had any of my leaders do in the past. She said she didn't specialize in my struggle, and so she referred me outside her organization to Dr. Gardner.

This seemed a bit reckless and random from what I was used to from spiritual leaders. My leaders in the past were very suspicious of outside help, and they watched their own leaders with painful scrutiny. It wasn't a big deal to Chaplain Mary, but I was shocked that she so quickly admitted she couldn't help me and then referred me outside her organization.

My theology that had been reinforced by my child abuse had me believing I had no free will. Dr. Gardner convinced me that I had free will by profiling my place in my dysfunctional abusive family. I was the youngest of five and the very act of me wanting to overcome the abuse threatened the family structure. I was accused of being a troublemaker by my parents and three of my siblings because I challenged the abusive structure. I was very curious, and I wanted to overcome the darkness that was holding our family back from happiness. My family would talk like they wanted to get better, yet their actions were apathetic at best.

Dr. Gardner encouraged me to read the book, *Healing the Shame That Binds You*, by John Bradshaw. This book showed my position in the dysfunctional family. It profiled me and my siblings. It helped me to understand why my brothers and sisters were resisting me and my effort to overcome the abuse. Dr. Gardner is also an expert on cults, so he helped me to understand my dysfunctional family and the rigid roles we played to survive.

Chapter 15—Scapegoat

My healing journey started when I was convinced that I am valuable. This set off a domino effect of causation. I could finally see why I had struggled so hard to survive in life. I was unwittingly part of a conspiracy to cover up my parents' lack of character.

Just the very nature of my character threatened my parents' values. I love the truth, and they love power and status. My curious nature and inability to compromise my values caused a huge headache to my parents. All of their children were expected to do their part and cover for my parents' character defects while they continued to pursue selfish ambition. My life was the thread that threatened to unravel everything my parents were working so hard to cover up.

I was carrying my parents' shame and guilt because I was convinced that it belonged to me. Confronting my parents and holding them accountable for abusing me moved that crushing shame and guilt from my head back onto the ones who deserved it. All of my parents' children were expected to continue the conspiracy of deception.

My mother and father were con artists by nature. They would work together to scam people out of their money. My mom is a very smart woman who is addicted to power and control. She is an abused woman; however, she has played the helpless role to gain power over her children and her husband.

My father used violence to get what he wanted and my mother used my father to get what she wanted. My mother was the brains behind the muscle. I liken my parents' marriage to the old Greek saying, "The father is the head of the family and the mother is the neck that turns the head."

I started seeing a cycle in my parents' marriage unfold over time. In order to control my father, Mother would push my dad to beat her up. She would accuse him of being less than a man and a weakling, a poor provider. My dad would finally lose it and attack her. My mother enraged my father to the point of violence. My mother saw that she could do no wrong in the eyes of witnesses after her husband was labeled a big, bad wife abuser. She became the quintessential victim, which assured her innocence in everyone's eyes.

My father would be overwhelmed with regret and shame for his terrible actions, and he would immediately move to make things right. He became putty in my mom's hands. I noticed we always lived where my mom wanted to live, and my mom always got what she wanted. Mom was manipulating father into abusing her because it was a small price to pay for absolute control over him. He idolized my mom, and she used this to control him.

Most of my life I had seen my mom as an innocent victim. When I started to value myself, though, I asked myself a burning question. Why didn't my mother ever have faith enough to trust that Jesus would rescue her from the crime of domestic abuse? Why didn't she do what I had done, and have the courage to confront her abuser? Why weren't her children enough to give her the courage to put her own life at risk and challenge this abuser? These questions led me to a painful conclusion. I realized that my mother is an extremely intelligent woman who used people to get what she wants. I felt betrayed and hurt that I had been duped for most of my life.

I saw now that my mother was using the "abused wife" persona to cover for her lack of character. She was not a prisoner of my father after all. She could leave at any time. She had absolute control over this man, and she was clearly the one in charge.

I had been trying for years to get anyone in my family to seek professional help, and so I was shocked when my mother told me that she did. My mother's indiscretions came to light when she told me about

an abused wives course she completed. She told me about the last step
of the class, which is where a person came in dressed like the Grim
Reaper. The Grim Reaper laid his scythe on the ground and the women
in the class were to step over that scythe, signifying that they would no
longer be afraid of death to the point of being completely controlled
anymore.

She told me this story before I had confronted either one of them.
Only after I confronted my father did the memory of this story come
to mind. After I had settled the score with my dad, my mother became
the focus. I realized that my mother was more interested in her selfish
ambition than in protecting her children from an abusive father.

I had bravely faced death down just like the abused women in that
class. This assured me that my mother had been told what she needed
to do, and it wasn't an issue of her being confused anymore. My mother simply wasn't interested in losing control over my father. She was an
abused woman, but she was not helpless.

As I continued to reflect on my parents, I saw the dysfunctional
yet working relationship they had formed. It was much like the infa-
mous couple Bonnie and Clyde. They worked together to get what
they wanted. It was gross and dysfunctional, yet effective. I realized my
mother had picked my father over me. She chose to keep me in the
abuse over letting go of control of Father. She should have protected
me.

My mother saying she was weak and afraid was not a good enough
excuse to me anymore, because I had faced the possibility of being
killed by my father when I confronted him. She should be held to the
same standard. Jesus conquered fear of death when he died on the cross
and came back to life. My challenge, as a believer, is to persevere in the
face of certain death, trusting there is an afterlife. I am to live as if God
is good and in control, not to live in fear. I am to live by faith.

Chapter 16—Cruel or Confused?

My siblings have all been coerced into this conspiracy of selfish ambition and disregard of God by my parents. I believe some of my siblings have embraced my parents' values knowingly, but others are just confused. Only God knows who is cruel and who is confused. I can't possibly know the answer to this question. All I know is that, either way, my siblings are not safe, so I moved to confront them last.

My oldest brother, John, is quite pleasant to be around. He is seven years older than me. When I was younger, he would share all of his wonderful interests with me. He was absent a lot throughout my younger years. Later, I found out he had a secret that would most certainly get him killed by my father. This is most likely why John was reclusive and stayed to himself. He was by far the sibling I felt safest around.

My next to the oldest brother, George, always carried the burden of covering for father. He felt it was his personal responsibility to fill the gap where my dad came up short.

I admired George's ability to work hard, yet he had a tragic flaw where he would self-sabotage. George had been deceived by mother and father. They saw in George his absolute dedication to serving them, and so they took full advantage of this. They gladly gave George their responsibilities with no remorse. George became addicted to compliments and affirmation.

Because George refused to see his father and mother for what they were, he became addicted to the notion that his mom and dad were good people who ran into hard times. They were certainly not bad or evil in George's mind. If George was to see that his parents didn't love him and they abused him, then it would mean he was unloved, and so the self-sabotage prevailed out of a sense of wanting to feel valuable. Like a magnet, George is drawn to those who take advantage of him because he is still trying to save his twisted parents, and in the end, his value and reputation.

I believe George saw me as his responsibility, in a fatherly way, so our relationship was doomed from the start. George would use shame, guilt, and scowls to cajole me into line. I couldn't shake the "fatherly" George, and he wouldn't have it any other way. He saw it as his personal responsibility to correct and train me. I felt sorry for George and his devotion to our parents, and so sometimes I would play along. George and I could never have a healthy relationship because he felt he had power over me and that I should respect that and obey him. George was too addicted to our parents' words of affirmation to treat me like an equal.

I was really glad that Nellie was a girl. Nellie is my oldest sister. She adopted my father's way of using intimidation to get what she wants. Nellie is not a complicated person at all. If she were a guy, bigger and stronger, she would have been more dangerous to me. Nellie would use the threat of rejection as a way of controlling those around her. Nellie is a bully.

When Nellie and I collided, she would take my parents' beliefs about me, that I was a lazy, no-good bum who wasn't to be taken seriously at all. According to Nellie, I was a fool, a jester to be laughed at and not to be taken seriously. Nellie knew she was mean and had no reservations about this. She saw intimidation as a completely acceptable way to get what she wanted. Many times Nellie and I laughed together, but it was usually at my expense. I have to admit I played the part of fool to get along with her. It was better than being alone, I guess.

Sally and I spent the most time together because we were closest in age. Sally was very sweet and nice. She was fun. We played together often and were stuck at home for hours with no supervision at all. Sally was kind, giving, yet tragically had no boundaries, so she was naïve as well.

Sally was an excellent server. She always was the first to try to help out. She bent over backwards to serve others. It was a great part of who she was. She was delightful.

Sally despised herself for being naïve, and so as we grew up together, over time, she began to get harder and harder. Unfortunately, somewhere along the line she traded her sweet self for a meaner self. To compensate for her weakness, she began to hang on to being right and a know-it-all.

She admired Nellie for her ability to reject people because Sally was completely incapable of boundaries. She accepted everyone, even bad people who would be abusive to her. She was merely playing out what she saw our mother do.

Sally continued to get harder as she deluded herself into thinking that being meaner was the answer. Sally threw out her good qualities of being serving and gentle and kind, along with the terrible qualities of being naïve and codependent. She filled the empty hole that was left with bitterness, grandiose pride, and religiosity.

Sally is still a victim of abuse, but she has deceived herself to believe she has overcome it. She is totally unwilling to address her inability to challenge those who are mean to her. In reality, she has a victim mentality that she has camouflaged with religiosity and grandiose-pride.

Chapter 17—Beyond The Law

Dr. Gardner had me read a book called *People of the Lie*, by M. Scott Peck, M.D. This book on human evil convinced me that I had free will. I was an abused slave as a child, and so it was only natural that I would believe I had no free will. My father ruled every waking moment; only his opinion mattered. My father made it clear that my sole purpose was to serve him. My mother reinforced this by encouraging me to always find ways to make Dad feel good.

At Bill Baker's church, I had to work to gain God's acceptance. Leaders didn't like talking about the fact that once you are saved, you are always saved. There was a fear that if people really understood their salvation was secure, they would use it as an excuse to rebel. But the very concept of "once saved, always saved" delivered me from the burden that Bill Baker placed on my back.

Also, I had read Rick Warren's book and studied it twice, and I realize now why it didn't profoundly affect me like so many others. I believe that *The Purpose Driven Life* gets people saved, but it doesn't show them how to live in freedom. I believe this, because I learned I operate better as a believer when I understand who I am, not what I am supposed to be doing. *Purpose Driven* begins with the premise that there is something you need to do which leads into burdens and works. The opening line of the book says, "It's not about you." As an abuse victim, this was not a profound statement. I believed life was not about me. I was trash.

What helped me to freedom was focusing on who I was rather than on what I am supposed to be doing for God. I prefer to say "identity driven" life, because this does not create performance anxiety, which only leads to extreme distress. As I started to look at the scriptures with a focus on who I am in Christ and not what am I supposed to be doing, I learned that Jesus was interested in my human rights and freeing me from the slavery of a burdened, unhappy life. I learned that Jesus doesn't expect me to white-knuckle anything at all. As I began to understood my identity in Christ, a new compelling force showed up in my life. For the first time, I wasn't doing things because I should do them, I was doing things for God because I wanted to do them. Wow. Revolutionary to my poor burdened soul.

Pastor Bill sold the idea that the people are to serve the church when Jesus, clearly, stated that the church is to serve the people. In Mark 2:27 Jesus said, "The Sabbath was made for man, not man for the Sabbath." I began to understand that Bill Baker's church was an abusive system. I read *The Subtle Power of Spiritual Abuse*, by David Johnson and Jeff Van Vonderen. This book profiled Pastor Bill's church. It was a very natural move for an abused and neglected person to gravitate toward an abusive church.

My identity in Christ says I don't have to *do* anything to be acceptable. I am completely perfect and valuable because Jesus said so. I used to see myself as a sinner, and now I have learned to see myself as a saint who sins from time to time.

It is all about emphasis. It is better to emphasize the fact that I am a saint than it is to talk about what a sinner I am. Bill Baker's followers were caught in a guilt-ridden belief system that said they were sinners who needed to be rescued by their leaders. The popular lexicon in an unhealthy church is for people to talk constantly about what terrible sinners they are. I found out that Jesus wants me to focus on what he did for me, not on my mistakes. Whatever I focus on will be my master in the end.

Pastor Bill had a perfect theology. He always had the right answer for everything. He always had the right answer, but he never had the loving answer. Bill was highly intelligent, but he was unable to apply the correct answer at the appropriate time. He was knowledgeable, but not wise in giving personal direction. He was a gifted teacher, yet he was a poor pastor and counselor.

What Pastor Bill did well was to teach me about the law. He taught me where the handrails are in life so I wouldn't stumble blindly into unnecessary pain. That was good, but the problem was that it stopped with the law. I later discovered that Bill Baker was showing me the handrails as to not fall, yet he was also stopping to worship the handrails. The Bible clearly states that "the Law Kills but the spirit gives life." (2 Corinthians 3:6) The law was comforting at first, but over time it has a strangling effect because it is purely performance based.

I have learned now that I am not above the law, but I am beyond the law. The law is no longer an issue for me, because I understand who I am in Christ. I realize that Christ freed me, and so I don't want to do anything to hurt his feelings.

My life has become about a relationship with Jesus Christ. Jesus is not a rigid task master expecting me to serve Him with no thought to my own happiness. Jesus wants to understand me. He wants to hear all of my complaints and then surprise me with an unexpected answer far beyond my expectations. It has taken me forty years to be able to trust Jesus, and now I can finally admit He is both good and in control.

The law still applies to me. I have respect for the law, but I have absolutely no reverence for it at all. The law is a tool in God's hands; it is not God Himself. I now understand what Jesus meant when he said, "My yoke is easy and my burden is light." (Matthew 11:30) God is not a hard man for a hard world. He gives life to those who sincerely seek him and love the truth.

I know now what happened when I was saved as a child. I was a good person who reached out to a good God for help. That's it. That is my story of salvation. There are other stories, but this one is mine.

There were never any demons that harassed me or possessed me. Those were the different broken parts of myself struggling to get along with each other. I was a confused and divided individual. Abuse had shattered me into several different rudimentary parts that warred with each other, all the time, in an effort to protect myself. The fact that I believed I wasn't valuable kept me paralyzed against any victory at all in my life. My life truly was hopeless.

I had been living with terror all my life. Terror had damaged my brain. My brain from the time I was a child had only operated in the fight, freeze, or flight mode. I was always in survival mode, never being able to use the upper half of my brain, which is for making executive decisions. I am now in the process of trying to heal this damaged part of my brain. My brain knows how to survive, but it has a difficult time knowing how to thrive.

I never believed I would ever be happy. I am happy now for the first time in my life. I have peace. In light of my newfound confidence, I moved to confront my father, my mother, and my siblings.

Chapter 18—Stand

I never had follow-through in the past. Each time I confronted my siblings and challenged them to take the abuse seriously, they resisted. I would appeal to them, with all of the new information I had learned, to stand with me and confront Mom and Dad for their abuse and neglect.

Time after time, I would try to make a case for challenging our parents, and time and time again they would get irritated with me and argue with me. I would point out obvious crimes where our parents had abused our human rights. They would then begin to accuse me of being too harsh. I would assure them that I learned these approaches from the experts, and then they would begin to argue with me.

At the same time, they would share awful stories where they were bullied by Dad or lied to by Mom. They would share a story about the abuses, then they would resist me, saying I was being unreasonable. I wanted all of us kids to stand up together against the human rights violations that had happened to us. I was outraged, and deep in my heart, I wanted us all to stand together and overcome the damage that had been done.

All I found was resistance. They would rationalize away the crimes against them or they would say that they were over what happened and healed. Ridiculous. You can't heal a wound by saying it's not there.

I would argue for a long time, and the longer I went on, the more resistance they would put up. They would get angry when I would use words like child abuse, neglect, unloved, or con artist. Our parents were all of these things, yet my siblings accused me of going too far with my accusations.

I would be accused of being selfish, unloving, and mean in my approach. They would admit these awful stories and then turn right around and protect Mom and Dad from my accusations. They would choose to keep the abuse a secret and call me an antagonistic trouble-maker. They would pick our abusers over my suggestions. I began to understand that they were actually protecting our parents.

For years I thought they were confused and that I had to help them understand the extent of the damage inflicted on our lives. When I started to see myself as valuable for the first time in my life, I began to see that they were not confused at all. This was a conspiracy, on their part, to hide the abuse and make me think I was crazy by discrediting anything I said. They knew what I said was true, but they didn't ever intend to expose the abusers.

Being treated this way all my life was making me crazy. For years I wanted to kill myself because I struggled with the belief that I was the problem. I was told I was the problem by my dad and my brothers and sisters all my life. I struggled tremendously with shame and insecurity. I seemed to be the only one who was compelled to seek justice. The shame of the family all rested on my head because I was the only one standing up to fight against the abuses.

I was terrified that, just maybe, they were right about me and that I was the problem. If this were true, the only honorable thing to do would be to remove myself from everyone's life by suicide. I had been told I was a loser my whole life, and for the most part I believed that. This belief rendered me powerless to stand my ground. Misdirected shame had me paralyzed.

I was kept preoccupied with my own hopelessness. I never stood my ground when I argued with my family. I would fight, and fight for them to see the abuse for what it was, but I would give up because I needed their validation. I had too much shame to take my own word for it. I needed them to affirm what I was saying so it would make it true. Self-doubt rendered me helpless. I thought of myself as hopeless, and so I needed their endorsement to make the abuse true. My word wasn't enough.

Either the abuse happened and I have a good reason to be struggling so hard in life, or my dad was right about me being a hopeless loser. I was tormented by these two scenarios. Was I an antagonistic bully and troublemaker like my father, or was I a good person who was a victim of a horrible crime? I didn't believe I was a valuable person, and so I was at the mercy of shame and hopelessness.

My siblings certainly weren't going to validate my claims of horrible neglect and child abuse because that would expose their own shortcomings and weaknesses. They desperately wanted to keep up the facade that they were in control of their lives and not victims. Being a victim definitely cramps your popularity and standing in society. They wanted to appear perfect. No one had shame, and so I decided to carry the shame for everyone. It almost killed me. Many times I have held a loaded gun to my head with my finger on the trigger, thinking I would do my wife and everyone else a favor if I put a bullet in my brain.

My dilemma was that I got saved on the premise that I am guilty, yet I am getting better on the premise that I am innocent. I needed to revisit what being saved actually meant to me. After some self-reflection and research, I found my answer.

My definition of sin was wrong. I liken my experience to how the word "sin" is used in archery. To "sin" in archery means you have missed the whole target altogether. The arrow has landed nowhere near the target. It has nothing to do with my character when I miss the target. God was not getting me to admit that I am an evil person—He simply wanted me to know where the true path to freedom is. For me, it was simply that I was lost and Jesus showed me the path. I was a good person lost in a cruel wilderness. It is not a character issue. It only becomes a character issue when I deny God and reject His free gift of salvation.

Before I was saved, I was living in sin, but I was in no way rebellious. I was ignorant of God. I was a good person, so when I was told about

Jesus and what He did, I loved Him right away and accepted Him, so I was saved.

The churches I went to growing up told me I was rebellious and a sinner. Being an abused child, full of shame, I accepted that I was rebellious and bad, which was not true about me. I was a sinner (missed the mark altogether), but I was certainly not rebellious.

The church had admonishment in the message of Christ, and it was not appropriate for my situation. Some people do need to be told they are sinners and rebellious, but those people are the types who are causing trouble for the rest of us. That message is for the guy in a rough motorcycle gang or the thief or the chronic liar, the swindler or the con artist.

I should not have been put in a category with the mean and cruel people. I was a clueless victim, innocent of anything sinister. I was simply living in chaos, oblivious of Jesus until I was told about Him. I was an innocent child who accepted Christ and was saved; never rebellious.

When I admitted I was a sinner, I was simply admitting I am a finite human being in need of the God who created me. I was admitting that I am not God and that I want Jesus to help me to become all I was meant to become. I admitted I was living in sin, which meant I was not in relationship with God. I was admitting to the absence of God's way in my life; no more, no less. I was ignorant, but in no way sinister.

The PTSD diagnosis, focusing on my identity in Christ, and the different experts I was seeing, gave me the validation I needed to finally settle on the conclusion that I was a victim. I am an innocent person who was horribly victimized. I decided in my heart to believe I was valuable.

This was the tipping point that finally started my healing after forty years of self-hatred. After peeling away the layers of all the people that hurt me, Jesus was still there, telling me I was infinitely valuable and that nothing and no one could take this away from me—not even myself.

When I had blamed God for being cruel toward me, it was a case of mistaken identity; my father deserves that accusation. Jesus was always for me, and it was a conspiracy of evil that was trying to discredit Him in my eyes. I became unstoppable after I grasped that I was valuable. I only needed myself and God to validate myself.

A few years before, I had confronted my father about the abuse, in person. I was terrified. I asked him about the abuse and he admitted to all of it. He even said he was sorry. But when I told him he needed to make things right, with defiance, he said, "I don't have to do nothing."

After confronting my father, I noticed that nothing changed for me. I didn't understand why, when I had finally confronted my father, I was still miserable. I didn't realize it at the time, but my father had confessed his crime but he was unrepentant about it.

When I confronted him, I was still hoping he would finally see how much he had hurt me and that he would break down and work to make things right. Until he did this, I would be in bondage to the abuse. I needed him to validate my experience or I couldn't get better. I was still his slave, hoping my master would change his evil ways so I could live a good life.

I didn't know this at the time, but I was completely at his mercy. I didn't have the ability to stand up for myself because I still believed I was a bad person—selfish and full of sin, undeserving of anything good. I saw myself as a sinner, not a child of the one true King—at least, until this very last time I confronted my father.

I took up where I left off with him the last time I had confronted him. I had already done everything except for holding him accountable for abusing me. He made it clear that he didn't owe me anything, so this last time I finished what I started. I called him on the phone and told him he was unwelcome at my home. told him that I would hurt him real bad if he ever came to my home uninvited. I reminded him of the time I had knocked him out to let him know I was serious, and then I hung up on him.

Feeling valuable for the first time in my life helped me to see the extent of the horrible crimes that had been perpetrated on me. It gave me sensitivity enough to feel outrage at the very thought of what had happened to me. For the first time, I had complete clarity about the crime, and I could move decisively.

I finally got the justice my heart was crying out for after all those years. I felt God's pleasure on me in that moment. I kept waiting for God to sweep in and rescue me, but I had come to realize he wanted me to have the satisfaction and self-empowerment of experiencing the justice first hand.

I could hear my father threatening me as I hung up the phone on him. I immediately went to my local police station and put in a report about my father. I told them I was afraid for my life because my father might come to kill me.

Being afraid of dying is what kept me from confronting my father and finding closure. When I finally faced death down, fear of dying no longer had a hold on me. Fear dissipated after I was honest directly to my abuser.

Soon after, I directed my attention to my mother. I called her and told her she had been a terrible mother and that she owed me compensation. She coldly exclaimed that the abuse and neglect were good for me and that I should be thanking her for preparing me for this cruel world. Then she went so far as to take credit for any victory I was experiencing. After I got off the phone with her, I felt a weight lifted from me. I finally confronted my mother about never protecting me. This was empowering. I then cried my eyes out at the realization of who my mother really is. I finally accepted the truth of my sad, abused childhood—that I was despised and unloved.

I had never dreamed of saying these things to my parents in the past, but I can see now that I was betraying myself for not being totally honest with them. A lot of my self-hatred came from knowing I didn't have the courage to stand up for myself. Most of my self-hatred and disgust came from the shame of not having the courage to stand up when my rights were being trod upon. The whole time, Jesus wanted me to stand up for myself. I had faced death down when I confronted my parents this last time.

I had learned what the Bible meant when it said to "stand." I decided to petition my brothers and sisters again to confront the abuse, only this time I would stand my ground and not seek validation. I warned them that if they did not aggressively confront the abuse with extreme prejudice, they were only passing the hurt on to their own children to deal with.

I sent them this letter:

"I am writing this to you in the hope that you will change your stance on Hank and Cassie. I have forgiven them, I pray for them, I love them, and I pray blessings on them. I am choosing not to be in relationship with them because they are what the Bible calls 'bad company.' Their values do not line up with my values.

"Hank is mean, jealous, vengeful, cruel, petty, and a bully. Cassie is not nurturing, cold emotionally, neglectful to her children, a chronic liar, and two-faced. They are parents who threw away their 'parent card' to pursue their own selfish desires, and they are still guilty of this today. They want the privilege of being father and mother without taking the responsibility of their terrible actions. They want privilege without taking responsibility.

"This would all be no problem if Hank and Cassie were repentant. I have been pursuing Mom and Dad most of my life, hoping they will change and take responsibility for their behavior. I have confronted Dad on his behavior and he said, specifically, that he has no obligation whatsoever to make things right with his children. He said he asked Bill Baker [pastor of Trinity Church in Dallas, Texas] about turning back to the Lord and that Bill's answer was unacceptable. Ask Dad about this if you don't believe me.

"Hank is a man who defies God and chooses to go his own way; Cassie is also unrepentant. Hank and Cassie know what they should do and they refuse it. This is not a case of ignorance or miscommunication or misunderstanding. Dad and Mom know exactly where they are, and they stand in defiance to the Lord. In Luke 9:5, Jesus instructs us to reject people who reject God: 'If people do not welcome you, shake the dust off your feet when you leave their town, as a testimony against them.'

"Cassie is just as rebellious as Hank. She has pretended to be the weak one all these years. Mom is neither weak nor ignorant. Hank and Cassie have been using the 'good cop-bad cop' scenario on their children to get control over them. Hank and Cassie are in rebellion and do not want to be rescued. They have been witnessed to time and time again. Even if they are not saved, you should move on because they are defiant against God.

"The best way to call Hank and Cassie to repentance is to move away from them. Leave them to their idols. Rejecting them is the best way to bring them to repentance. You should not chase after people who are in rebellion against God. All you can do is offer them the message, and if they reject it, move on.

"If you continue to pursue them, they are leading you, you are not leading them. You are called to lead, and sometimes leading is walking away. In turn you are exposing your children and spouses to the same manipulation and abuse. It is easier to pursue Mom and Dad than it is to appropriately reject them. Do not invite these people into your home. You are allowing the same poison that hurt you to then be heaped on your children and spouses. I guarantee that each one of you have stories of when Mom and Dad abused your children and your spouse. Start protecting yourself and your loved ones. The easy way out is to try to 'save' Mom and Dad, but the more difficult route is the better way.

"Matthew 10: 34-39 supports what I am telling you. This passage basically talks about putting the love of family members over the love of God; this is what Jesus said.

Do not suppose that I have come to bring peace to the earth. I did not come to bring peace, but a sword. For I have come to turn a man against his father, a daughter against her mother, a daughter-in-law against her mother-in-law. A man's enemies will be the members of his own household. Anyone who loves his father or mother more than me is not worthy of me; anyone who loves his son or daughter more than me is not worthy of me; and anyone who does not take his cross and follow me is not worthy of me. Whoever finds his life will lose it, and whoever loses his life for my sake will find it. (Matthew 10:34-39)

"As long as Dad and Mom refuse to acknowledge the past for what it was and to take responsibility for it, stay away from them. You are only dragging yourself and your families into their mess. I am sure that Dad and Mom feel bad about what happened and they wish things were better. Dad has even told me he was sorry. I accepted his apology, but he still refuses to change his behavior. This bad behavior is still happening today. I am not just speaking of the past; I am talking about the present behaviors as well. Hank and Cassie are both unrepentant.

"I suggest that until you see a drastic change in the way they behave over a few years, only then should you consider allowing them back into your lives. There is hope for Mom and Dad. At this time they must prove to me that they have changed and that they want to take responsibility for their past.

"The best way for them to start showing they are sorry is to start sending money to each of us until we say it is enough. Money is what Hank and Cassie worship right now. They would have to send money, and whatever else I think they need to do, in order to win me back.

I am a child of the King, and I refuse to be abused by them—or anybody else, for that matter. Respect yourselves and restore your self-confidence by having strong boundaries and standards in your lives against cruel people who would harm you.

"If God is asking you to reject Mom and Dad for his sake, would you do that? Make up your mind about whether you are going to follow Hank and Cassie or God. You can't follow both. The pathway to peace is to move away from Hank and Cassie and toward God. Teach Mom and Dad how to follow God by your example.

"If you need help doing this, give me a call and I will help you with details and specifics on how to do this in a kind and loving way. It will be best for you and the ones you love to get out of the bondage of trying to save Mom and Dad or even just hoping they will change as they heap abuse on you and your family. I have a tremendous amount of peace in my life because of this. God is blessing me with happiness.

"Jesus Christ in Luke 14:26 said, 'If anyone comes to me and does not hate his father and mother, his wife and children, his brothers and sisters—yes, even his own life—he cannot be my disciple.'

"I have sent a copy of this to John, George, Nellie, and Sally. Thanks for taking the time to consider this. I love you guys. Jack Flynn"

I came to understand that a person can only be for or against the abuse; there was no middle ground. I warned them that silence is consent. I told them they were actually protecting the very people who had abused their human rights. Still, after my letter, they rationalized away my parents' abuse and belittled my pain and hurt. They justified their apathy by trivializing the effects of the abuse.

Chapter 19—Safety First

I finally had to give my siblings an ultimatum to protect myself because they were sympathizing with my abusers. This sympathy made them dangerous to me. They were dangerous because they were not concerned with punishing evil. There was no justice in their world. A world without justice is ruled by the wicked. I really didn't want to lose them, and so I increased the pressure by listing out firsthand all the damage I saw in their lives. I was hoping they would finally be disgusted with the abuse enough to join me in my fight against it.

If they weren't going to agree with me, I knew I had to break fellowship with them. I explained that it wasn't enough for my parents to say they were sorry. They needed to be held accountable. I told them I was not ever going to see my parents again unless they started to compensate for the damage they had done—in action. I knew now that if we didn't challenge our parents, they would never respect us. My parents could say they were sorry all they wanted, but until they move to make amends, the buck stops with me.

My brother, George, told me he never wanted to see me again. George got angry when I told him he would pass the abuse down to his children if he never confronted it. Nellie said she never wanted to see me again after I started posting on Facebook that I was coming out about Dad and Mom's abuse and neglect. Sally started trying to convince me that I was being unforgiving and spiteful. Sally told me that Jesus was forgiving and never rejected anyone. Sally did not believe in the death penalty and thought Jesus was a pacifist. She was all about grace in her mind. She told me Jesus would not approve of my strategy.

I see Sally's theology as an attempt to cover up her own fear of confronting her abusers. Sally used religiosity to cover up her lack of faith. Sally has twisted what the Bible says. She does not have the courage to confront her abusers, so she has fashioned a theology to camouflage her character defect. Her belief that Jesus would never reject someone protects her from the terrifying task of holding her own abusers accountable. You show me a pacifist, and I will show you someone who has no justice in their world.

Many Christians believe Jesus was a pacifist because he never fought back with force. Jesus didn't fight back because he was to be a sacrifice for the sins of all mankind. "What would Jesus Do" is a reasonable way to live until I am expected to be like Jesus and lie down when I am attacked. Jesus was not a pacifist; He was a perfect sacrifice. I am not called to die for all the sins of mankind; Jesus already did this. Jesus was fulfilling a prophecy by letting Himself be killed.

I am to use self-defense when I am attacked. The "turn the other cheek" verse, according to the NIV Bible, only applies in insult. It has nothing to do with being physically assaulted. Jesus certainly expects us to defend ourselves with lethal force if needed. I believe that, unless God intervenes in the moment in a miraculous way, it is okay to kill a person who is trying to murder me.

Some people misquote the sixth commandment, Exodus 20:13, and believe it says, "Thou shalt not *kill*." Exodus 20:13 is truly saying, "Thou shalt not *murder*." Killing and murder are completely different. God was saying not to maliciously take a life. Killing a bad guy in the Lord's eyes is perfectly okay.

What my sister lacked in her theology was justice. God loves justice. An often misused passage is where the Bible says, "An eye for an eye" in Leviticus 24:20. "Eye for an eye" is not a revenge verse. It is simply illustrating that a punishment shouldn't outweigh the crime. If a person takes the life of another for malicious reason, then his life should be taken. The death penalty is about justice and doing what is only fair.

All this being said, when I knocked my dad out, Jesus was actually pleased with my response. I am sure He is pleased with me holding my abusers accountable today as well. Some Christians are called to lay down their lives, while others are called to kill to bring peace.

I have been accused by my sister, Sally, of embracing violence and being just like my father. She made the argument that you can't defeat violence with violence. I did struggle with this issue for most of my life. I was afraid because I had used violence just like my father, it meant I was turning into the same person. I was wrong.

The *American Heritage* dictionary's definition of violence is "physical force exerted for the purpose of violating, damaging, or abusing: Crimes of violence." I was stopping a crime by using physical force. I did not use violence. My father was using violence, but I was righteous in my action to stop my father with physical force. It is not a crime to stop a crime. Good warriors are not violent people; bad warriors are violent people. I am righteous. Knocking my dad out, I believe, made Jesus proud of me.

Proverbs 20:30 says, "Blows and wounds cleanse away evil, and beatings purge the inmost being." This is saying that God sometimes uses physical force to stop a tyrant. According to the New Matthew Henry Commentary, Proverbs 20:30, "Many people need severe rebukes." Sometimes bullies need to get beat up before they will stop hurting people.

Jesus is a warrior. In Revelations, Jesus returns to put an end to evil. Revelations 19:11 says, "I saw heaven standing open and there before me was a white horse, whose rider is called Faithful and True. With justice he judges and makes war ..."

Jesus is the rider on the white horse. This passage is after Jesus has been a perfect sacrifice for all mankind. He returns with an army to kill His enemies and bring justice. Jesus is in favor of just wars that liberate the oppressed. A world without justice is a world subject to tyranny. To say that Jesus is a pacifist is to say that Jesus is not a just God.

My belief that Jesus is a warrior was confirmed when I found and read a book called *Another Man's War*, by Reverend Sam Childers. It is a true story about a man who took up arms and fought a madman to save children in the Sudan.

This book jumped out at me on the shelf at Barnes & Noble bookstore. I was struggling with fear that Jesus was passive and uninterested in bringing my abusers to justice. I needed a God who was a warrior because I could not respect the Jesus I had been taught about. I loved Jesus, but I struggled to respect him. God needed to be strong for me, and Sam Childers was the man of God I was hurting for.

Sam Childers' story inspired a major motion picture called *Machine Gun Preacher*. I was further shocked to realize that Sam Childers was going to be not far from me at a showing of his movie. He was raising money for the victimized children in Sudan, Africa. This was no coincidence. God perfectly orchestrated this whole scenario.

My wife and I immediately drove about forty minutes away to meet Sam Childers where we watched *Machine Gun Preacher* and got to meet his wife and friends who travel with him. God had affirmed in me that he loves justice and that he fights evil with extreme prejudice. This gave me the courage I needed to embrace that side of me that is brave and willing to do whatever it takes to fight bad guys. I was born with a killer instinct, and that movie helped me come to the conclusion that a killer instinct is a gift in the right hands. I was affirmed in my use of force so many times to defend myself. A person can righteously kill for the sake of peace. My warrior side was acceptable to Jesus because He is in fact a warrior as well.

My healing started after I seized justice for myself. I showed faith to the Lord when I confronted my abusers in the face of my fear of being killed. I needed to experience Justice to find closure. In the past, I stopped short of confronting the abuse because of my fear and confusion. I have overcome that fear now so I am experiencing freedom for the first time. I understand now that Jesus died to say that I am infinitely valuable. Jesus died for my human rights.

Matthew 10:34-39 explains the challenge I had before me:

> "Do not suppose that I have come to bring peace to the earth. I did not come to bring peace, but a sword. For I have come to turn a man against his father, a daughter against her mother, a daughter-in-law against her mother-in-law—a man's enemies will be the members of his own household. Anyone who loves his father or mother more than me is not worthy of me; anyone who loves his son or daughter more than me is not worthy of me; and anyone who does not take his cross and follow me is not worthy of me. Whoever finds his life will lose it, and whoever loses his life for my sake will find it."

I had to turn away from my family in order to follow Jesus. I was hoping they would follow me, but they didn't take me seriously. It was a very difficult and painful decision, but I had to turn them away until they decided to respect me. I forgive my dad, my mom, and my siblings. They cannot come back into my life until they decide to take the abuse more seriously. I prayed for them and I wish them the best, but nobody is ever going to abuse me again without serious consequences. I love myself too much now to allow my human rights to be violated and do nothing.

Chapter 20—Counter Culture

I struggled with rage most of my life, and this rage was destroying me because it was misdirected. I finally had to go against the tide of the culture and blame my parents. I was told that blaming my parents was wrong and that it was an excuse to not take responsibility for my own problems. I was told that my parents did their best and that I should only be grateful. The fifth commandment about honoring your father and mother was quoted.

I believed it was wrong to blame my parents, until I realized that it was my parents' fault that I couldn't work. The child abuse inflicted by my parents had deeply damaged me and left a huge mess in my life that I was forced to clean up. I struggled with feelings of helplessness, suicide, powerlessness, PTSD—the list goes on. I was blaming myself for these problems.

I started to see that irresponsible parents were abusing the fifth commandment to honor your father and mother. This verse became a get-out-of-jail-free card for them. It is being used by parents to skirt their responsibility to clean up the hurts inflicted on their children. I don't believe God put this commandment in the Bible as immunity for abusive or neglectful parents. No one has immunity from sin.

I have always honored my parents. I honored them to the point of slavery. Honoring parents is not even the issue when they have hurt their children. I still love my Mom and Dad, but that doesn't mean I should cover for the crime of child abuse. I should take a hard line when expecting compensation. God is simply saying never to degrade or demean their value as human beings and to show them respect.

Unfortunately, dishonest parents have taken liberties with the definition for what is dishonorable. Dishonorable, in their evil minds, has come to mean *anything* that makes them feel uncomfortable. Parents are subject to the truth just like children. Parents have the exact same value as children, and they have the same human rights. Cruel parents abuse the fifth commandment. My blaming my parents and holding them accountable is right, good, and true.

If I don't give my parents consequences and hold them accountable for their actions, this only allows the abuse to continue unabated. It is only natural that I would begin to hate myself and grow sick because I was humiliating myself by protecting my abusers. There is no possibility for healing, closure, or justice when I protect my parents by not confronting them. Whether parents are guilty of a small little white lie or something as terrible as child abuse, the fifth commandment does not apply in these situations.

The only thing I am responsible for is to not fall into bitterness, hatred, or revenge. I can, however, pursue righteousness and justice because God loves these things as well. I can love my parents while at the same time have extreme prejudice against their lies. I can bring them to justice and expose the lies. I can also refuse to allow them into my life.

I can use what my parents did to me as an excuse not to be able to work because of the psychological damage. If someone paralyzes me from running into me with their car, I can use what they did as my excuse not to be able to walk anymore. If someone asks me why I can't walk, I can say that I blame the person who was negligent in the car that hit me.

Unfortunately, invisible wounds don't get the same respect that visible wounds do, so this has brought a lot of unfair accusations against me. "I can't work because my parents abused me" is equivalent to saying I can't drive my car because it was so badly damaged. There is absolutely no shame in this. My challenge is to guard my heart against hatred, bitterness, and revenge.

Chapter 21—Self Love

I first began to heal after I confronted my family and held them accountable with consequences. I am still open to having a relationship with them, but they would have to agree with my belief about the abuse and move, in action, to convince me. I value myself now, and I have standards that people must meet in order to spend time with me. I love and respect myself too much to allow chronic liars into my life.

The healing started to flow when I got a new perspective on my same old problems. Nothing has changed except my perspective. I went from valuing myself through what I do to valuing myself for who I am.

I am just as valuable when I am sleeping in to miss work as I am when I am having a banner day at work. The homeless person on the street has just the same value as the president of the United States in God's eyes. I need God's perspective on the world, not humanity's.

I cannot work because I am disabled. I came to believe that this is not a character issue at all. I am a victim of abuse, and I need to make the proper adjustments to move forward. No amount of white-knuckling was overcoming the damage.

The prevailing attitude in most churches is, "You are saved; now, what are you going to do for the Lord?" I believe they should say, "You are saved, and so now let me help you understand who you are."

Serving God should never be a burden at all. Serving should come out of the overflow of love for God. God does not need us to serve him; He's God! God wants us to be in relationship with Him and for us to know Him intimately. Jesus wants us to know that He suffered to free us from burdens, not to buy our service.

Now that I understand who I am in Christ, my addictions have become less powerful. In the past, the thought was that my relentless sinful nature was the problem and I needed to suppress the urges with all my strength. I needed to show God I loved him by not giving in to my lust.

This was absolute torture. It had the opposite effect that I wanted; it actually increased my desire to sin. I would inevitably sin and then feel horrible because I showed God that I didn't love Him. I could only feel guilty and despair about my failure. I was mired in the quicksand of performance.

When I started to grasp that I was already saved and I didn't have to try harder, my prayers changed from, "Help me, Jesus, to keep from sinning" to "Help me, Jesus, I am going to sin and I can't help it." Jesus showed Himself each time I sincerely prayed this prayer. Through trial and error, over time, I began to get better at surrendering to Jesus for help.

I was taught in the past that repentance was to make a 180-degree turn away from my sin; that I had to make it up in my mind that I wasn't going to do this behavior any more. This doesn't work.

Repentance became, for me, the ability to release myself into the care of Jesus. It wasn't anything I did on my own power. I simply let go and trusted that Jesus was going to rescue me.

I was caught in a cycle of white-knuckling to try to stop sinning. I learned that in order to stop a bad habit, I must replace it with something good and pure. My addiction began to lose steam, over time, as I focused on good things. I couldn't stop my addiction when I focused on stopping the behavior; what I found I needed to do was overwhelm it with good. I followed Philippians 4:8 when it says, "Finally, brothers, whatever is true, whatever is noble, whatever is right, whatever is pure, whatever is lovely, whatever is admirable—if anything is excellent or praiseworthy—think about such things." I overwhelmed my addiction with reading Scripture and prayers as well as by focusing on the new person I had become in Christ.

As when a person beats cancer, I am only in remission when I overcome my addiction. It could come back at any time. I need to overwhelm it by meditating on my identity in Christ. Feeling bad about sinning is bondage; feeling good about my standing in Christ is the cure.

The Catholic Church reformer Martin Luther has a quote that I love. He said, "Be a sinner and sin strongly, but more strongly have faith and rejoice in Christ." I like this quote because the first part is inevitable; I will sin strongly no matter what. But the second part is the solution: "[M]ore strongly have faith and rejoice in Christ." It reminds me not to get trapped into despair by my relentless sinning, but to continue to move forward into the belief that I am free.

I still sin from time to time with pornography, but I find it doesn't have the same hold it once had on me. Now I know what to do when my lust becomes too much for me. I immediately confess my sin, tell a good friend, and I make my access to that sin more difficult. Most importantly, though, I find relief in meditating on my identity in Christ. I am saved. I am going to heaven. I can't mess that up. I have security, and so I refuse to let shame and guilt drive me into hopeless feelings of depression and despair. I am free, so I should live as if I am free. It does great dishonor to what Jesus did on the cross when I allow myself to become paralyzed by shame and guilt. Jesus doesn't want me to feel bad for sinning, and so I don't. Even if I sin, confess, sin, confess a million times over, each time I confess, I should live as though I am free and shake off shame and guilt. Focus on things above to pull yourself out of things below.

My logical mind told me I would descend into a deeply depraved state of bondage to my lust if I didn't resist the addiction by my own power. That didn't happen. It was a huge step of faith, and God intervened to rescue me.

I changed my belief about myself. I was no longer a "sinner saved by grace." I was now "a saint who sins from time to time." This is very subtle, but huge in its impact. I am a good person because I chose Jesus and He chose me. We chose each other. This is what I mean when I say I have a relationship with Jesus Christ.

Relationships are spontaneous and always changing. I have learned never to be rigid about my beliefs. I am going to heaven for eternity, no matter what, so I need to stop giving credence to my sins with guilt. God does the hard work, and I just show up and trust him that, no matter what happens, all will work out for the best because I am a child of God. I am no longer the son to my earthly father. I am a son to the one true powerful God of the universe. I am valuable.

Now I talk with Jesus on a regular basis, and I share everything with Him. I give Him requests and I trust that, no matter what happens, He will bless me beyond my expectations. I hold every request with an open hand because I know now that He is good and wants the best for me.

It has taken me forty years to trust God because I was terrified He was like my earthly father. My earthly father did do a few things right, but God is that, and infinitely more. I have learned how to surrender to God, and so it has minimized my addictive struggles. I still sin, but sin doesn't define me at all anymore. I am free, so I am determined to live as if I am free.

Chapter 22—Justice or Revenge

I am very happy at this time in my life. I am in relationship with Jesus Christ. I still have unanswered prayers that tell me I am a fool to trust Jesus. I guess I am not so crushed by unanswered prayers now because I have walked with Jesus long enough to believe there is a heaven. I see now that earth is the doorstep to eternity. I won't spend much time on the doorstep; it's a short distance.

I can do this. I can make it. I am not here on earth to have all my dreams come true; I am here to understand who Jesus Christ is and trust Him to have all my dreams come true. Jesus wants me to feel good and be happy. I believe this now.

I was born into chaos. I found the law, which created stability, but then it started suffocating me and I was still dead inside. Exasperated, I collapsed into the arms of Jesus Christ. For the first time, I met people who accepted me just the way I was and worked hard to listen and understand when I talked. They had no agenda for me and they worked hard to understand me.

These people included the professional PTSD counselors; Chaplain Mary Theresa the grief and loss expert; Dr. Gardner, the expert on cults; and all of the other friends of good character who run with these people. These good people are my relationship with Jesus Christ.

Being abused, I was a city without walls. I had poor boundaries and discernment. My only boundary was my willingness to use physical force to protect myself or those I love. I am still very proud of that boundary, but now I have a few more tools in my discerning tool box.

I learned to discern good people from bad by asking myself if they feel safe. The word "safe" allowed me to tap into that portion of myself that was scared and too afraid to reveal itself. I read the book *Safe People: How to Find Relationships that are Good for You and Avoid Those Who Aren't*, by Henry Cloud and John Townsend. The weaker, more sensitive parts of my personality became convinced it was safe to come out when they knew the "Spartan" part was only going to be respectful and safe.

The shattered parts from the abuse began a dialogue with each other for the first time in my life. I had a conversation with the fierce Spartan warrior part of myself and told it to stop tearing me down and to stop using any kind of degrading words as to try to protect or motivate myself. As I changed the dialogue with the protective parts of my personality, the more creative, sensitive sides were free to come out of hiding.

I was suffering from being a one-dimensional personality. Now I have a deeper pool to draw from as my parts synthesize. My parts are beginning to cooperate with each other. I have smoother transitions between my different parts, and so I feel whole for the first time in my life.

I no longer see the world as a desolate wasteland of cruelty and selfishness. I do believe a cruel world still exists, but there is also a world of truly safe and kind individuals who are sincere and loving. Yes, much of the world is horribly cruel and dangerous, but there is a stronger force in the world that loves peace, mercy, and justice. I have experienced this first hand for myself, so I am convinced the whole world is not a loss.

There is hope. Not everyone is a hypocrite. People only have to be willing to take responsibility for hurting me and they can be my friends. I don't expect perfection from others, but I do demand character and integrity. Jesus Christ is the only person who I can rely on to never hurt me. My full allegiance is to Him alone. People will let me down, but Jesus has proven himself to be 100 percent reliable.

Holding people accountable for their actions is confused when it is thought to be revenge. There is a huge difference between justice and revenge. Justice, according to the *American Heritage* dictionary, is "the upholding of what is just, especially fair treatment and due reward in accordance to honor, standards, or law; fairness." Revenge, however, is "to seek or take vengeance for (oneself or another person)."

Justice is a loving effort to bring compensation to the victim. It is also an effort to make sure the punishment doesn't outweigh the crime. Justice shows self-control and consideration to a person's humanity. All men and women are made in the image of God, and so respect and care must be given not to degrade a human being or be cruel, no matter how terrible the crime. It is not revenge to give a murderer the death penalty.

Revenge, on the other hand, is when the punishment outweighs the crime. It is taking matters into your own hands and using excessive force to punish the perpetrator. It is not being fair when judging another. Revenge involves no self-control and it is negligent in its attempt to right a wrong. Revenge is carelessness.

I have been accused of revenge by my siblings. I have in no way been excessive toward my parents. It has been a painstaking process of self-reflection, research, and seeking counsel for me. I love my parents and I hope the best for them, but I would be a fool to cover for their crimes. I am following the Bible by seeking justice and mercy. My hope is that removing myself from their lives will encourage them to take responsibility for their crimes.

It is my responsibility to protect myself and hold my abusers accountable. I am rejecting them with the hope that they will suffer from not seeing their youngest son, and so this will cause them to repent. It also protects me from further harm in the process. If they never repent, I am protected from people who are cruel and do not have my best interest at heart. I am safe either way.

I have wanted to take revenge, but I know better. Revenge hurts the perpetrators and me. I am determined to do this God's way so I can assure my greatest chance of having peace and happiness for myself and my wife and daughter. Revenge is intermittent and hurts those I love. It is foolish to take revenge.

Chapter 23—Simply A Gift

The warrior in me loves the chivalry ethos. I am determined to do what is right, honorable, and true for the sake of all the parties involved in the child abuse. I am not only interested in being right, but more importantly, I want to do the loving thing. The symbol of a knight best showcases my character. I have fought, and always will fight to protect the weak. I would sooner die than dishonor the Lord Jesus Christ.

I believe Jesus Christ is the only path where a person can find the power to stand on being valuable. Any other form of self value requires a person to earn that value through effort. People cannot effectively deem themselves valuable apart from the power of Jesus Christ and His free gift of salvation. All human beings have value whether they believe in Christ or not, but accessing the unwavering power to stand on that value is another matter.

The key lies in the free gift a person needs to reach out and receive from Christ. A person without Christ is alone and out of relationship with the one true God. Not having access to Jesus Christ forces the unbeliever to find self-value through his or her own effort. There are limited possibilities, yet this person will never experience the peace and life the Bible speaks about.

Believers can also fall into the trap of performance if they are ignorant of their standing in Christ or if they decide to rebel. A person can be saved, yet, living as if he or she is *not* saved. A believer has access to the power to change, whereas the unbeliever has no such assistance.

One of the enemy's greatest strategies against the saved is to convince them that Jesus Christ dying on the cross to save them was too simple of a solution. The enemy says Jesus Christ didn't go through suffering and dying on the cross for you to sit around on your behind and not do anything. It is an attempt to distract believers from seeing their standing in Christ by using shame. Shame is a devastating weapon that the enemy uses to great effect. The enemy simply says you should be ashamed for putting Christ through such horrible suffering and convinces you to do more than what Jesus has done. The Bible calls this mistake "works." Works is a trap for the shame-ridden, and the power hungry are quick to take advantage of the shameful to use their guilt to fuel their own selfish ambition.

I was a victim of believing the lie that what Jesus did for me was not enough. This lie was reinforced by my parents and church leaders out of their selfish ambition. I was convinced I was hopeless, and this made me an easy target for guilt. Guilt had rendered me powerless and easily controlled by the establishment. I was defensive and exasperated with trying to prove to others that my experience had credence. I was caught in a trap of always trying to justify my actions to others when the whole time, as a believer, I had been justified by Christ. I just needed to stand on the truth about the abuse. Jesus had validated me at the cross.

I was declared free of blame and absolved of any misplaced shame or guilt when Jesus died on the cross. I have been justified, by Jesus, to demonstrate good reasons for my actions. I do not need another's permission to declare that my rights have been trampled on. I can stand alone with confidence in the face of any authority and declare that I am to be treated with dignity and respect. I matter because Jesus says I matter; it's that simple. I no longer need another person to justify my beliefs. I can stand alone in the confidence of Christ's power. This is my definition of true freedom.

I have also been told the Bible says it's wrong to judge people, and so I do not have the right to judge anyone. When the Bible says in Matthew 7: 1-5 not to judge, it is simply saying not to be a judgmental person by nature. Matthew is telling us not to go around looking for fault in others.

Making a judgment call and being judgmental are two totally different approaches. God certainly wants us to use good judgment. This passage is saying that when we do judge, we must not judge rashly or with the desire to cause trouble. I am not being judgmental.

Jesus has walked alongside of me, from the time I was saved, making sure that my life was orchestrated in such a way as to arrive where I am now, in freedom and understanding. The way I have learned to live now is to hold everything I want with an open hand. I need to trust that God knows best in every situation. I lay my desires on the altar and ask God to answer them. My challenge is to surrender my goals, dreams, and fears to Jesus.

I have now discovered that when I was saved, all the vital work was done. I no longer need to carve out an existence for myself and my family in the world. My only task now is to live day to day within my limits, trusting that God will meet all of my needs and wants.

In my prayers, the sky is the limit for what I pray for. I don't hold back. Each time I have seen God answer a prayer in my life, it is always a surprise and above and beyond what I hoped for. I still have some prayers that are not answered, but I resist the urge to worry because I have walked long enough with God to see that He wants me to be happy.

Chapter 24—Ambition

I see now that the time I have on earth is short and that when I die it will most likely be at an inconvenient moment. Even when people know someone is going to die, it still feels sudden and unexpected. God is intimately involved in people's lives, whether they want him or not, moving the human race in a specific direction. We are too limited to see the bigger picture.

I have noticed, though, that the less ambitious I become and the quieter I make my soul, the more I see God in the world. Through my difficulties, God has taught me to be still and see him working in the world. My biggest hurts have caused me to cry out to God. My hurts have compelled me to go places I never planned to go.

As I have been broken down by my troubles, God has used them to change my perspective on the world. I have learned to embrace my weaknesses and surrender to God's process. I went from a warrior who never gives up to a warrior who only gives up to the Lord Jesus Christ.

What is important to me is also very important to God; however, He knows me better than I know myself, so I have learned to yield to Him more quickly. I do not bang my head against closed doors so much anymore. I have learned to knock a few times, try the doorknob, and if it doesn't open, I move on. I trust God to give me what I want.

I understand now that calling Jesus my master has absolutely no limitations to my happiness. I agree with Oswald Chambers, who said, "To have a master means that there is one who knows me better than I know myself, one who is closer than a friend, one who fathoms the remotest abyss of my heart and satisfies it, one who has brought me into the secure sense that he has met and solved every perplexity and problem of my mind." This is the definition of Jesus being my master that I choose to believe.

Ephesians 3:20 says, "God is able to do far more than we would ever dare to ask or even dream of—infinitely beyond our highest prayers, desires, thoughts, or hopes." I am discovering this is true as I have the courage to relax into my struggles and stop fighting them. God is surpassing my expectations after long difficult trials.

Jesus said in Luke 9:23, "If anyone would come after me, he must deny himself and take up his cross daily and follow me." This verse is telling me to be aware of my limitations and to work within those limitations. I must deny the temptation to be more than I am, to be bigger than life. I like the old army advertisement that says to "be all you can be." I am not to be *more* than I can be; that only creates pain and hardship.

What I do is I pray ambitiously and live humbly. I wait for God to bless me. In the meantime, I take care of what is directly in front of me and surrender to contentment. I am to be patient and wait on the Lord, trusting that He will bless me beyond my wildest dreams.

There are people who work very hard who are rich and people who work very hard who are poor. God raises people up. A man can work hard, but God sets up the opportunities for him to excel. God lines up opportunities that succeed, not men. This is why becoming famous or super rich is elusive to those who are very talented. Only God raises people up, and it is a Christian's responsibility to be quiet and look for God to prompt him. I prefer the Bible's definition of ambition in 1 Thessalonians 4:11: "This should be your ambition: to live a quiet life, minding your own business and working with your hands, just as we commanded you before."

When I was young, I mostly made decisions based on my heart or how I felt about a situation. When I learned more and was immature in my faith, I made decisions based on logic and rationality because I was told my heart couldn't be trusted. Now I wait for both my heart and my head to align before I move forward.

Chapter 25—Meanwhile ...

In relationship to my current pain and sufferings that have not been resolved, I fin d it is my perspective on that pain and fear that helps me cope. Fear can increase my pain exponentially. When I start focusing on trying to make myself whole, worry and terror begin to abuse me. Trying to become a balanced, happy individual creates anx iety. When I try to balance my life, I become like a tightrope walker straining against invisible forces that are constantly pulling me down ward. Balancing something is not easy. Fighting against gravity and fear brings a tremendous amount of anxiety, which increases my pain. I have fallen into the trap of performance, thus the rise of performance anxi ety. Performance anxiety starts a downward spiral of despair and hope lessness.

According to the Bible, my aim is not to be a whole and balanced individual. I believe Jesus wants me to experience him. I need to trust that the wholeness was taken care of when Jesus died on the cross. I am only to suffer a little while on this planet. Jesus gave me the free gift of eternity in heaven.

I won the prize when I accepted his free gift of salvation. I have been saved already. Why would I waste my time trying to save myself all over again by my own power? God is simply using my trials to help me understand who He is and what He is doing in the world. When I die, I get to receive my full inheritance of everlasting happiness—free of any suffering.

My trials are making me more like Jesus as I surrender to the process and stop fighting out of fear. I know it makes me feel wonderful when someone likes me enough to put their trust in me. I believe this is what Jesus wants from me: to trust Him enough that He can start blessing me with understanding. Jesus lets me peek behind the curtain of heaven each time that I trust Him. I get to see that everything is going to be fine and that God knows what He is doing. He wants to be my perfect father that I can come to about anything and He will make it right.

This is an imperfect world, and I should not see it as unusual when something terrible happens to me. As a believer, though, I have the confidence that a good God is directing my life. God wants me to love Him so much that He gave me a choice to *not* love Him. I have a choice. It is a terrible choice, but nonetheless I have one.

I can choose to trust Him or I can choose to be bitter and miserable to spite Him. The temptation is to get revenge against God by refusing to cooperate with Him. My life can be defined by trusting God or fighting God. I can choose hate or love. Choosing love is a choice to surrender. Choosing hatred and bitterness gives a person a false sense of being in control of the outcome.

The choice of bitterness makes me a part of the problem and not a part of the solution. Each time I am faced with a trial, I choose to be a part of the solution, not a part of the problem. Choosing the solution makes everything go more smoothly for me and for those around me.

Each time I am faced with an impossible choice, I pray the prayer in Mark 9:24: "I believe, I believe, help me with my unbelief!" God mysteriously answers my prayer each time I cry out to Him. Some would call this a coincidence, but I find a lot of coincidences happen around me when I cry out to Jesus.

I have learned to embrace my struggles and stop pushing them away. I keep my hopes and dreams flexible enough to change at any moment. I trust that God really does know me better than I know myself.

Through trial and error, I have developed this relationship with Jesus. In time, He has proven Himself reliable and trustworthy.

I came to realize, also, that whatever I love the most in my life eventually comes to have power over me. I am a limited, created being and this is an unavoidable part of that identity. Whether a person believes in God or not, this is an inevitable outcome.

I may have lost my biological family, but I have been adopted into God's family. Jesus has become my perfect father who knows best. Because of my parents' abuse, it has taken me forty years to finally come to the conclusion that my parents abused me, not God. I, like Jesus, was abused for doing nothing wrong. I take comfort in knowing that Jesus suffered in innocence like me.

I have come to understand that people can be evil apart from God. God was there from the beginning. Even when I was terrified and being abused, God had a plan to use me to bring these evil people to justice. Yes, God could have saved me in a moment, but I choose to believe He wanted me to see that evil runs deep, yet Jesus runs deeper. The seemingly indiscriminate pain I was subject to was ultimately held in God's hands, working it out to a greater purpose. My pain has gone from meaningless to purposeful, which is much more easily accepted.

I already do this to myself regularly where I break myself down in order to build myself up. I lift weights to strengthen my body. There is a period where I actually make myself weaker by breaking down my muscles. Yet, when these muscles heal, they are even stronger than before.

I endure the pain and soreness because I know it will pay off in the long term. My suffering is bearable because I can measure the pain against the benefit. I know that, with perseverance, there will be good results.

God is doing the same thing with my life on a much larger scale. I can't measure the cost-to-benefit ratio—at least not until years later when I have hindsight. Much like my controlled efforts to bring about physical strength, God puts me through trials to strengthen my faith.

God is maturing me and preparing me for much larger blessings than my limited mind can fathom. When I was saved, this is what I signed up for. In coming to terms with the loss in my life, I have come to discover that God is going to compensate me for the damages. Some of the compensation will come in this lifetime and the rest will be paid in full in the next life. I have nothing to worry about; I am saved, saved from my trials and losses.

Chapter 26—Conspiracy

I have learned to wait on God. He is quite spontaneous in His blessings. I allow myself to be surprised. I have stopped trying too hard to control or make sense of things. This only brings grief, anxiety, and frustration.

I take care of whatever is in front of me, and I let God surprise me. It has become a very exciting life for me now. God loves to surprise me and see me smile. I stop stressing and wait on God. God hates it when I suffer, but He hates it even more when I give into the conspiracy of evil.

The conspiracy of evil is trying to convince me that I am all there is, that mankind is teetering on the brink of a bottomless pit, and that love is for fools. Evil is trying to convince everyone that God is a liar and there is no hope. The enemy wants us to degrade our humanity by settling for less.

The comfort with evil is that you can predict what will happen next. Evil gives a sense of control to those who rely on it. The comfort from evil comes from being able to predict the outcome in every situation. It is easy to assume that nothing will work out, and most of the time you are right.

It is easier to destroy than it is to create. That is the attraction to the power of evil. It is the easier road to comfort in predicting the outcome. I find hope much more painful than despair. With despair, I know I will be miserable, but with hope I have no idea what to expect! Despair has its own comforting message. Despair equals more despair, and somehow knowing that outcome is comforting. It is a deathtrap that only God can break when we ask Him for help.

Abuse has seemed to knock me way off target when it comes to finding my purpose. However, I don't believe this is the case. Abuse has served as a platform for me to tell others about how God rescues those who trust him. God has allowed me to understand there is something much larger going on in the world.

Evil and suffering can be redeemed. Evil is aggressively storming all that is good and holy. I have learned that evil is under God's control. God is not directing evil, but He is more powerful. God is simply giving me the opportunity to choose. I can choose selfish ambition or faith in a good father.

I have a long way to go, but for the first time in my life, I want to live. I am horrified at the idea of killing myself, and this feels wonderful. I never dreamed I would love myself as much as I do right now. I have moved from believing I am trash to believing I am priceless. This is a major accomplishment for me. Now I can stop surviving and start thriving. My healing has only recently started, and so my next challenge is to avoid the performance trap. I am not sure how much time I have left, but I find peace in knowing that no matter what happens, everything will work out because my God is good and He is in control.

My challenge now is to constantly remind my body that the danger of being abused is not imminent. When I get startled, my body starts a chain of events I have learned to ride out. I understand now that when I am afraid, I overreact. My body and parts of myself want to act "as if" the abuse is happening today.

In a moment, I can return to the world where I once lived, a world where I am terrified for my life. There was a time when I was a slave to an evil, abusive man who gave no thought at all to my rights as a human being. That time has passed.

It had been trained into me since birth that I have no rights and that I live for the service of my leaders. Now that I have my new sense of value in place, I can begin to train the slavery out of myself. A slavery value system was trained into me, and so now it is only a matter of time before I train a new set of values into myself.

This new set of values includes my standing in Christ. Times are hardest when I lose sight of who I am and begin to live out of the habits of the past. When I am startled, I begin living in a fight-or-flight state. Everything becomes the enemy and I can trust no one. In an effort to self-protect, I retreat into a bunker where I become fiercely independent. The "bunker" is where I isolate myself through physical and emotional distance.

I find myself overreacting to the current situation because, in my mind, I am that little helpless child who is abused. I have learned to pull the "ejection seat" lever too quickly and too often. This makes for unneeded pain for me and for those I love.

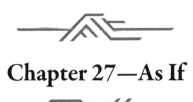

Chapter 27—As If

My body has become a vehicle that only operates on adrenaline. I have an all-or-nothing approach to situations. I am either crashing or I am going a hundred miles an hour. A pattern of violence and fear has shaped my body to operate only in crisis.

Normal life feels like a death sentence to me because my body is not wired to handle cruising speed. I am out of my depth when it comes to marathons. I feel like a sprinter trying to run a marathon. Pacing is not even in my vocabulary. I am a child of adrenaline and I need to train myself to operate on normal energy resources. I need to retrain my brain and my body to live "as if" there is no emergency. My trauma counselors are trained to help me with this effort.

At one time, I would have read what I just wrote and thought, "Impossible, never going to happen." That is because I could not grasp how valuable I am. I now understand that I am valuable, and that value can't be taken away. This new belief gave me a platform to begin working on what was once a pointless exercise. I tried getting better by my own strength and it didn't work. I stayed stuck. Now I am growing for the first time under this new ethos.

A lot of damage has been done to my body by operating only on adrenaline. I don't know the extent of the damage and I probably won't live a long life. I have mystery health problems and chronic pain. However, since I have started to see myself as a child of Christ, my chronic pain has gone down, along with my anxiety. I still have impossible moments where I despair, but they are growing fewer and further in between each episode. Suicide is no longer an option, because if I shoot myself, the darkness wins. I hate evil, and so I want to be around to make it suffer. I will fight evil with every sinew of my strength and wits until the day I die.

I am not saying I could never be in a situation where I would want to kill myself again. That is very possible, because I love deeply and so I hurt deeply. I am great now and I don't see suicide in sight, and so I will continue to live boldly and courageously. I will not play it safe when it comes to living because I refuse to be afraid of death to the point of being paralyzed.

I am not working now and so I have decided to write my story down. I am using this time to do things that bring me peace. Writing can bring up painful feelings, but it is also therapeutic. Writing helps me to channel the toxic fallout from the abuse. I have been journaling for years, so I finally decided to organize my experience into a cohesive story to help me make sense of my life.

I can be a very nervous person. Any kind of excitement has a negative effect on me, whether it is a good experience or a negative experience. My mind can differentiate between good and bad, but my body is different. My body sees any kind of excitement as dangerous. This is very frustrating when I want to do something fun. A couple of the things I like to do are to have conversation with my wife at a coffee shop or enjoy time by myself. There are a lot of things I would like to do, but my body will not cooperate. I find myself at home most of the time, reflecting on my life.

I have a lot of social anxiety, and so I isolate myself to cope with it. I am an introvert by nature, and so I seek out alone time as much as possible. My mind is always busy with trying to make sense of my life, and so I am actually quite active on the inside. I am not a physically active person by nature, yet I am in deep thought most of the time.

Isolation can be a double-edged sword. I do struggle with loneliness from time to time, but I see it as a small price to pay for peace. Sometimes I try to find creative ways to be around people. I like being around busy places where I am anonymous.

My latest project is to create safe places in my life. A safe place is where there is no phone, people, or unexpected interruptions of any kind, a place where I can have a couple hours of solitude. I read a book, journal, or talk to God. Other times I may listen to music or watch a show. It is a place where I can do anything I want. I find I need to exercise my free will in order to strengthen myself. I don't mind being by myself for extended periods of time; I see this as a strength. I can meditate and center myself. I refuel for the times I have to be around others.

Chapter 28—Too-Simple Solution

A s for demons, I feel I must believe they exist by faith. I don't be-lieve demons were ever a problem for me. I don't believe true be-lievers can directly be harassed for any extended period of time. I be-lieve in demons because I believe in Jesus. It's that simple. It is my belief that if a demon ever did try to bother a believer, the moment the be-liever called out to Christ for help, the demon would immediately flee. This nonsense of trying to exorcise a demon with great effort is ridicu-lous.

I certainly believe that demons were a part of the problem with the sins of my family and the only reason they could hurt us is because some of us were not believers and others were ignorant of the power they have in Christ. The church I went to in Texas oversimplified prob-lems and had no respect for how complicated people can be.

Because Pastor Bill had little respect for individual rights and no intimate relationship with Jesus Christ, he had a catch-all solution that was easy; any problem is a demonic problem. If you can convince your congregation this is true, it makes them more easily controlled. The members become dependent on their leaders because any personal problem they have needs to be brought to the experts in spiritual war-fare. Pastor Bill was not interested in empowering his members with the belief that believers ultimately answer to Jesus Christ, not our church leaders. Bill's eagerness to rule reached past individual human rights so as to assure his position as leader. I liken the old adage to Pas-tor Bill: "You can fool some of the people all the time, and all the peo-ple some of the time but you can't fool all the people all of the time." I am living proof of this. Do I believe in the demonic? Yes. Do I believe the demonic can personally antagonize a believer? No. It is not a major issue for believers when Christ is involved.

The apostle Paul had a "thorn" that he called a messenger of Satan that he could not remove. I believe that anything is possible because God can do whatever He wants. But considering a problem as demon related should be a last resort and then only the believer who is harassed can know for sure. Calling everything a demonic issue is being careless with one's personal responsibility to work out our salvation.

In the past I took the belief that most problems are demonic. I prayed all the time against the demonic in every situation. Since I self-diagnosed with PTSD and started learning about Dissociative Identity Disorder, I completely stopped praying against demons all together. My life has improved dramatically. I am happy for the first time in my whole life. I have never had more peace and joy. It has been years now since I stopped praying against demons. Life is good.

Now, when I become conflicted and I start arguing inside my head, I follow the mean words back to the source. The words I heard over and over again that conditioned me came from someone who was cruel to me. It is usually a part of myself that still falls into the trap of believing I am trash. I identify that part, and I politely ask it to stop being cruel and to start building me up. I thank it for helping me through the horrible times, but it's time it changes its message.

At one time I had to agree with my abusers about what they said or they would beat me to death. I agreed with the horrible lies about my identity in order to survive. When I agreed with my abusers, it went easier for me. I was too small and helpless to fight back, and I did this in order to survive.

I liken my experience to how elephants are trained in Eastern countries. As soon as a baby elephant is able to walk, it is leashed to a stake that is hammered three feet into the ground. The untrained baby elephant struggles and struggles against the stake, but it is too difficult to pull out of the ground. After many struggles, the baby elephant realizes it is just too much, and so it gives up. Years go by and the baby elephant grows into a full-sized bull. As a bull that weighs a few thousand pounds, it could easily pull the stake out of the ground. However, it has been conditioned to believe it is too difficult, so it doesn't even try to pull out the stake. They stay put, tethered to a tiny stick.

Much like that stake, the abuse has trained me to believe I am powerless and helpless. Situations that are very difficult for me are effortless to most others. I get overwhelmed and discouraged easily. I must recondition myself to believe there is nothing holding me back but a lie, a lie that I am helpless.

I remind myself today that I am no longer in that situation. I do not have to believe I am trash anymore to survive. I change the dialogue in my head from my abusers' to what Jesus Christ says about me. Agreeing with my abuser is called "Stockholm syndrome." Agreeing with Christ is drawing strength from my "born-again" identity.

Chapter 29—I Was Justified

I am at the beginning of a long, hard road because I have to recondition my brain to believe a whole new ideology. I have been conditioned most of my lifetime to believe that I am nothing and helpless. I am now at the beginning of my new self, or what I believe the Bible talks about when it talks about my "born-again" self. This is what Christ means when He tells me I am born again.

Every day is a battle to change the dialogue that has been conditioned into my brain. It is easy for me to forget my identity in Christ because I don't have much practice with relying on this new identity. I must undo the damage that was done, and this will take many years to achieve because it took many years to be conditioned. I must retrain my brain.

For the first time, I have hope because I finally have grasped what Jesus is saying when He tells me I am justified by His death on the cross. It was nothing I did on my own power. I had been declared free of any blame and made like Christ in His innocence. By justified, I mean I can stand on my feet in front of any accuser and look them in the eyes and tell them they are wrong about me.

Jesus took it a step further and adopted me into His family. I have all the benefits of being in Christ's family as a brother. I have received the full inheritance of the royal family. I am considered royalty, a prince like Christ. Christ's father is my father, the King of Kings and Lord of Lords. When I grasp this concept, I am unstoppable. I have been made righteous. My father is *the* King not just *a* king.

Every day it is my challenge to remember who I am in Christ. Sometimes I forget who I am or I start listening to the wrong voices and

I start living out of my old self. This can be devastating and very diffi-cult to free myself from. Therein lies my struggle at this time in my life. I am getting better at battling the lies. I can tell I am healing. I still have years to go, but I will continue to get better—better at understanding who I have become in Christ.

Chapter 30—Naughty Church

Corporate church has failed me, but the organic church is healing me. The church I went to in Texas told me that the church is not the building but the people. They were right in theory but not in practice. They prided themselves in believing that the church is not a building while the whole time limiting God with their contract and their rigid expectations to obey the leaders in that contract. There was no room for faith in their rigid expectations of the congregation, no room for a relationship with the living Christ. Micro-managing people squeezes out freedom. There is no freedom for Christ to be unexpected and surprising in His mysterious ways of speaking to His people. Micro-managing a congregation is simply self-protection. Fear leaves no room for Jesus Christ.

In reality, their idea of the church was those who signed their church contract for membership. They are guilty of squeezing God into the limits of a document. The local church is not only those who sign a church contract.

I have no problem with people joining a church and signing a church agreement. I only have a problem when the church only considers its people who signed the document as being in the local church. It is wrong when a document creates an "us-versus-them" mentality. Church leaders, and anyone for that matter, can't possibly know who is saved and who isn't. Only God knows the answer to this. The membership agreement in churches should not be used as a self-protection device. The contract should not be written up in fear or in a controlling nature. I do not believe a person has to be a part of a particular organization to be recognized as a believer.

I do believe that a true believer will seek out other believers so as to exercise their gifts in the Lord. This is good and healthy. Signing a church agreement, however, does not have any bearing on a believer's standing in the Lord. I volunteer my time at a local para-church ministry, although I am not on a church membership officially. Only a pastor who wants to selfishly control others would have a problem with this. I am quite happy with this situation, and I am regularly in contact with my fellow believers. In Matthew 18:20, Jesus says, "For where two or three come together in my name, there am I with them." If it is good enough for Jesus, it is good enough for me.

What was the church before it was nationalized? Roman Emperor Constantine, around 306 CE, was the first to nationalize Christianity. Before Christianity was nationalized, it was illegal and so believers met secretly in homes or whatever location they could find. When the church was nationalized, it gave the impression that it was now somehow okay to be a Christian. God didn't need the emperor's endorsement. The church was acceptable and okay long before the emperor declared it to be so. In some ways, I believe Christianity being nationalized was not good for the church.

When church was nationalized, it simply won a popularity contest and became cool to be in the church. This took the church in a whole new direction. It became a path to gain power, popularity, and control. All the sudden, the church leaders had overhead and they needed to pull strings to pay for their bills. That burden fell to the congregations. The church leaders stopped serving the members and the members were tricked into serving the leaders. The idea of church got horribly twisted into a self-serving monopoly.

In the meantime, Jesus got tossed aside by selfish ambition. Church government that doesn't know its place, I believe, is one of the tools God uses to squeeze out our "fear of man" and realize our needed independence on Jesus alone.

Church leaders used fear to drive me into their church membership contract. I was told I had to be a member of a local church or I would fall into debauchery and forget about Jesus. This has not happened to me.

As a believer, I can't help but seek out other believers. I am compelled to seek out fellow Christians for support. I no longer worry about being a part of a church membership because I am compelled to seek out believers regardless. Worry never served me well anyway. Fear only serves naughty church leaders, so I gave that up.

Chapter 31—Jumpy

The abuse has also stunted my emotional growth. On the outside, I am a full-grown man, while on the inside, I have the emotional stability of a scared child. I feel out of my depth in many situations that are banal. Ordinary situations that are of no great alarm send me into a panic. I have trouble learning simple tasks because I become overwhelmed with anxiety and feel out of my depth. I am quite intelligent, except when I am overwhelmed with anxiety.

When I start a new job and I have to learn something as simple as a cash register, I panic. As I am being instructed, my ability to retain information is drowned out by an onslaught of anxiety. I panic and grow confused. The more I am pressed, the worse I get.

I begin to sweat, and I have a hard time hearing because my heart is pounding so loudly in my ears. My socks, underwear, and shirt become soaking wet. All I can think about is running as far away as possible from the current situation. I want to hide in an anonymous place where no one will ever find me, and I hope to be forgotten. My ability to learn suffers tremendously.

Performance anxiety times a thousand. I can't help but revert back to when my father was trying to teach me something. It went like this. "Come on, boy, put the lug wrench on the on the nut and turn it." I would fumble because it was my first time. My father would go on, "What are you, stupid?" Father escalating: "You aren't worth the powder and lead to blow you up!" His eyes bulging and face twisted in disgust: "You will never amount to a hill of beans."

In the moment when I am trying to learn the cash register, I do not have this scenario with my father in the front of my mind. I may not even remember it. However, my brain senses stress and triggers these memories subconsciously. Now I am learning to self-reflect and hear this conversation with my father and change the dialogue from one that tears me down to one that encourages me and is kind.

This is very difficult and scary work. It is much like entering into a haunted house. I do not know what I am going to find, and I am sure it will not be good when I do find something. It is an awful and terrifying journey into my own personal house of horrors.

To take this horrific journey, my trauma counselors have taught me grounding techniques to keep me in the present so as to not lose myself in the past. I work on staying present in the room as I journey back to these memories. A trained professional is needed to help with this journey.

It is a painstakingly difficult task. It is much like trying to dig a hole in mud. The overwhelming feelings of terror are the mud that is thick and difficult to shovel. Like mud, the emotions threaten to paralyze me in a quagmire of pain and hurt. It is a difficult journey, and anyone who attempts it is a courageous person.

Doing this time and time again slowly brings the past into the present where it can be reframed in light of current circumstances. When I do have an episode and overreact in rage, I get stuck in what is called "trauma time." "Trauma time" refers to when I get stuck in the overpowering emotions of the past event in a current situation.

Chapter 32—Threat Level

The most painful "trauma time" feeling I experience is helplessness. Helplessness is terrifying. I feel totally exposed and vulnerable to be exploited. I always move to protect myself from feeling helpless with rage. Rage gives me a feeling of being in control. My rage compensates for the feeling of being exposed.

At one time I was tiny and helpless to defend myself, and this was humiliating and terrifying. I can easily get overwhelmed again when I feel slighted in any way, large or small. These are called "triggers." I need to also work on identifying triggers and begin a conversation with my old self to reduce the threat level.

I find that situations that only require a level two response can get a level nine response. This is out of a scale from one to ten. I need to talk myself off of the ledge by leaving the current threat and returning at a later time when I have had time to process the threat level. There are a lot of triggers, and this takes a grueling effort on my part. Even for a seemingly small incident, if I feel exposed and in danger, it can feel like trying to lift a sumo wrestler off of my chest to change gears and have an appropriate response. I have never had a sumo wrestler on my chest, but I imagine that's what it would be like. I have benched a few hundred pounds before, so it can feel as harrowing and dangerous as that.

I still find things to do that give me a sense of control. I still workout regularly and stay in shape. I hate the idea of being weak, and so I still train my body. However, I am much more effective now with results because I am not as desperate as I once was. I find it scary to get older because my body is becoming more fragile. I am over forty years old now. I can injure myself much more easily than before.

I find myself working harder on being smarter, and I have to let the physical strength take a backseat. I will always try to keep myself as physically fit as possible, but I am being forced to consider other alternatives to self protect. I have always been a formidable physical force. Physical fitness still gives me confidence to handle most situations. I have made coming up with creative solutions to protect myself a fun exercise.

I busy myself with preparing for emergency situations. It is fun to prepare myself and my family for natural disasters or social unrest. I keep food, water, and various other supplies in my vehicles and around the home. I like to organize and streamline supplies for disaster preparedness. I find this a fun and relaxing exercise that builds my confidence. I also do this to help alleviate the feeling of impending doom that I can be plagued with. This is one of the hobbies I have taken up that is fun and gives me a feeling of empowerment.

I find that my body runs at generally two speeds. I am either hypervigilant or I am crashing. This makes living a consistent life impossible. If I get excited about anything, I find I can't sleep even if I want to. I feel my body getting tired as the hours pass by; however, my brain is anxious and hyper alert. The anxiety keeps me up until dawn sometimes. Even though I am exhausted, I cannot sleep. It is a bizarre place to be. All I can do is ride the anxiety out until I finally crash. I find I then have a shallow sleep, awaking at the slightest noise. I sleep my best when I am alone in the house, although battling the shame of being in bed for so long can antagonize my sleeping as well.

Chapter 33—Snake Oil

I have been told by countless leaders and relatives that if I get a job, everything will work itself out. I was told that "guys are like trucks, they work better under load." This is completely false. I have taken job after job, fully intending to have a career and move up, only to find I cannot stop the cycle of hyper-vigilance and crashing.

Because I have a problem not being able to work, most people feel uncomfortable. They immediately go into fixing me when I say I can't work. People react as if I told them I was never going to walk again. They look stunned and then begin to try to comfort me as a way of making themselves feel better. They treat me as if I have a horrible disease they do not want to catch.

Most of my family and past friends see people as either useful or useless. A person who is producing is a good person, and a person who is taking is a bad person. There are only two categories for people. Either you are giving or you are taking. I hated telling my friends and family about my disability because I knew I would be put in the "useless taker" category. Human dignity and value are not even in the equation in a "pull yourself up by your own bootstraps" world.

Jesus is not asking me to pull myself up; He is asking me to believe I am valuable no matter what happens. If I try to pull myself up, the effort immediately breaks the access to Him working miracles in my life. It is not by my strength that I am saved, but by Christ's love. I find I perform better when I stop struggling to make myself important, and I relax into the reality that I am a limited being who is needy.

My disability has actually put me at an advantage over those who believe they have their life together and they don't need anyone. Being independent and self-sustaining is a fantasy. No such person that exists. Everyone is a needy individual in some way or another. We rely on the garbage man to come and take our garbage away. We rely on the water company to continue to send us water. We rely on hospitals when we are injured or sick. We rely on the Department of Transportation to keep our roads safe enough to drive on, and the list goes on. The American dream of fierce independence and rugged individualism can be a dangerous fantasy.

If we believe we don't need anyone, then we are blind to our limitations and headed for disaster and heartache. I now understand that when a new problem comes into my life, I merely need to make an adjustment. This says nothing about my value as a human being.

I have also been told that there is good stress and bad stress. I don't believe this either. There is only bad stress, and any stress is bad stress. When I work to minimize the stress in my life, I find that I work much more efficiently. Stress can't be removed altogether, but it can be minimized.

I find many people are workaholics because they are addicted to the adrenaline rush. Workaholics leave a path of destruction in their wake. Over-working is one of the addictive behaviors that is admired and rewarded in this culture.

In a funny way, workaholics are my arch nemesis because I cannot work. I am very jealous of those who can get up and go to a job every day. Workaholics gather together and complain about how they carry the weight of the world on their shoulders. They complain and complain, all the while believing the world would implode if they didn't go into work the next day. Complaining is a sneaky way of bragging about all the responsibility they have and how important they are. This really bugs me, because I cannot work for good reasons. This does not mean I am useless or somehow inferior. I struggle tremendously with feeling inferior, so I am very sensitive to workaholics and their tendency to pat each other on the back for their addiction.

I have learned that workaholics over work because they do not have the courage to face the relationships in their lives that demand attention. They are neglecting relationships in their lives with consequences that will be felt through generations of family. James Dobson said that kids spell love T-I-M-E. Workaholics are guilty of not loving their own families, which lead kids to all kinds of psychological damage. It is irresponsible and passes the buck onto the children or spouses. It also heaps unneeded abuse onto those who can't work. People should be grateful they can work and treat it responsibly as a gift and not as a right.

Chapter 34—Back in the Black

This book is a major milestone in my life. I have written it for a few reasons. It helps me to find closure with the nightmare I endured. Also, I hope it will create a sense of heritage for my daughter and grandchildren. I come from a broken line of people who chose selfish ambition over a relationship with Jesus Christ. This book represents the hard work I have done to establish a good reputation for myself and my family even though the odds were against me.

I have divorced my parents and most of my siblings as a means for establishing a platform of integrity that my daughter can use to carry on if she chooses. Luke 14:26 says, "If anyone comes to me and does not hate his father and mother, his wife and children, his brothers and sisters—yes, even his own life—he cannot be my disciple." Obviously, a good man loves his family. What Christ is saying here is that you must love Him more than any other person in the world. Unfortunately, I have had to make the choice to stay away from my parents and siblings because of their values. Not everyone has to do what I did, because each situation is unique. My family forced me to choose when they decided not to hold their abusers accountable. Jesus has rewarded me with a great deal of peace and understanding for showing my faith in Him. Yes, it is hard now, but I believe I would be lying down in torment if I had never divorced my birth family.

Now I can finally close this awful chapter of my life. I wanted to share my horrible trial as to testify that God is good. He allowed this horrible thing to happen to me, yet He has repaid me with an unshakable worldview that will help me endure every trial. I have an understanding about the world that goes far deeper than my dreams and desires. I see the bigger picture of life now, and God has won me over to His side.

God has been working very hard to let me know He had nothing to do with the evil that scarred me so deeply. I see now that I have suffered alongside Jesus. Jesus suffered unfairly, so he understands my being an innocent victim. God has suffered with me and for me. My time on this planet is not simply for me to get as much as I can before I die. I was created to have a meaningful relationship with my creator. Everything pales in comparison to knowing the one person who can make all of my dreams come true—the dreams I didn't even know I had until hardship exposed them.

Don't miss out!

Visit the website below and you can sign up to receive emails whenever Jack Flynn publishes a new book. There's no charge and no obligation.

https://books2read.com/r/B-A-MKMN-GOBMB

BOOKS 2 READ

Connecting independent readers to independent writers.

About the Author

Jack has spent most of his life digging out of the quagmire of self-hatred caused by child abuse and violene. He has moved from a desparate, anxious life to a peaceful, hopeful, and content self. On his jouorney to find peace and happiness, Jack was a leader in a Christian recovery progrem and earned his undergraduate defree in journalism and his master's degree in psychology. Jack has a special ability to articulate overwhelming and confusing emotions associated with being unloved and despised as a child.

CPSIA information can be obtained
at www.ICGtesting.com
Printed in the USA
LVHW111621020123
736049LV00007B/384